THE WEAVING OF MY TARTAN HEART

donelda macdonnell

Suite 300 - 990 Fort St
Victoria, BC, V8V 3K2
Canada

www.friesenpress.com

ISBN
978-1-5255-8632-3 (Hardcover)
978-1-5255-8631-6 (Paperback)
978-1-5255-8633-0 (eBook)

1. BIOGRAPHY & AUTOBIOGRAPHY, CULTURAL HERITAGE

Distributed to the trade by The Ingram Book Company

This book is dedicated to
Joan Campbell Ferguson
The gentle nag. Thank you for believing in me, thank you for the push.
I love you and you can't stop me!

Acknowledgements

Special thanks and much gratitude first of all to Joan Campbell, without whom none of this would have happened. Only she and I know the amount of encouragement she had gently put on me to believe in myself.

So very grateful to my first cousins Mary Janet, Marey and Duncan who fixed up the disaster of technical publishing stuff that I could not do—saving the day, just in time. What would I have done without you? Thank you so much.

To Steve Rankin, Margie MacDonald, Bob Martin, Colin MacDougall and Rob Martin for help with photography issues.

Photos of veteran's medals and prayer book, courtesy of Jerome MacDonnell.

To Carole Chisholm and Beth Ryan, my gratitude for your testimonials.

Thank you to Jeannie Kirk, old eagle eye, who saw this book happen twenty-five years ago. I don't know why she never mentioned it before this ☺.

To my wonderful, brilliant, creative and beautiful granddaughter Kaitlin Shears, whose exasperation with me led to this common comment *"Gramma! What did you do now?"* Thank you darling. I know how technically incompetent I am.

Posthumously, I want to thank Little Collie MacDonell, who always believed in me saying, *"Anybody could do it, but only a Weaver did!"*

And now the best for last. Franklyn Ferguson is a mentor, a counsellor, an inspiration, a Catholic sister and a friend. Your patience and encouragement have meant the world to me Franklyn. Together we developed workshops that would help many people. You mean the world to me Franklyn. I love and respect you.

TABLE OF CONTENTS

INTRODUCTION

The Weaving of My Tartan Heart offers a peek through the window of the author's thoughts. Vivid images of a time long past make the reader feel as though they are present in each scene. Stories of when life was simpler, and when respect for elders and tradition evokes a warmth you can feel deep in your soul—like a cozy woolen blanket. Donelda's nostalgia for those days reaches out and captures your heart. Some chapters are a tribute to her early days in the '50s and '60s, when time was spent just being a kid and people were resourceful. Those clear memories have tumbled forth onto the pages of this book to capture the tenacious spirit of the Cape Breton people. —Mary Janet MacDonald

What do *you* bring to the table?

The beginning chapter of this remembrance was written at Dalhousie University in 2003, following Professor Linda Wilson's assignment to each of us in class to develop an *Instruction Manual* about who we are as persons and who we will be as social workers. I came to understand that I could not do a self-assessment without first telling a story about my mother. So I presented an analogy of how my mother's devotion to sewing measured up to my perception of ideal social work skills. The chapters that follow are a tapestry of the materials and designs that unfolded from writing that first vignette.

My mother was Annie Margaret (Beaton) Mac-

Mabou Coal Mines: Warrren Gordon Photographic

Donnell and her people came from the beautiful Coal Mines in Mabou, Cape

Breton. Cape Breton is a little island in Nova Scotia, Canada, but most Cape Bretoners believe it to be the centre of the universe[1].

I am the daughter and grand-daughter of incredible women who, like myself, had difficult lives, my mother in particular. My father had returned from overseas, damaged by the violence of the Second World War. My mother could make or fix most anything but she was not able to repair the damage done to him by the terrible experiences of war.

My female relatives, like myself, were seamstresses born with the inherent ability to improvise, change, create, repair and produce incredible garments from scratch, without even using a pattern. My sister Ellen is an excellent seamstress and a lot more organized than I am. We both make wonderful quilts.

My grandmother, Ellen (Doyle) Beaton was a naturally skilled tailor. She had the God-given capability to see many possibilities in fabrics before she even began to feel the textures of them. Besides sewing for her own three children, she made her living fashioning men's suits. An admirable task even by today's standards, but even more so then, when done by kerosene lamp and foot-pedal sewing machine. She squinted by candlelight while stitching by hand or as she sewed with her Singer sewing machine. She mastered the difficult art of making hand-stitched buttonholes and sewn-down lapels. She made entire suits with lined vests, pleated pants and fitted jackets. In addition, she added stiffening and interfacing that required time-consuming physical labour and the mental ciphering of a perfectionist. A proficient and reliable presence of mind was required to cut and properly match the grain of the fibres in the materials.

Extra skills were needed to match the 'nap' of fabrics such as tartans, corduroys, or velvets. She told her customers what she needed in order to put a suit together. The people made the purchase 'in town' and brought the materials back to her. In her little house, overlooking one of the most picturesque places in the world, she laid out her plans and the fabric on her table once more to begin yet another project. No doubt my mother watched

[1] Ray Smith, *Cape Breton is the Thought-Control Centre of the Universe*, Anasi Press, Toronto, 1969. Ray Smith lived in Mabou until his death in 2019; he was waked at *The Red Shoe*.

her every move, bringing the items to her that she needed to complete the suit. Although she died in the 1930s, Ellen Doyle and her skills are still much admired by the older folk 'back home' in my village of Mabou. They will say she was known for being a respected seamstress and, more importantly, a fine person who helped everyone.

In turn, my mother sewed for her own eight children and for the people who brought their torn garments into her kitchen. Respect naturally descended on to her from Ellen Doyle's work ethic. But my mother earned her own credits. She never had a driver's license, so people brought their work to her. She did this amid the piles of children's clothing to be washed in the old wringer washer, and huge batches of bread to be baked in the wood stove, as her many children ran around her feet. She was always praying. I could always hear the familiar Catholic prayers being whispered as she sewed. Hail Holy Queen...Mother of Mercy.

I followed in these fine women's footsteps. My electric sawing machine was more modern and I too had the baking, all that laundry and the kids.

Recently, I spoke to an older woman whose life had been nicely touched by my mother. She proudly poured out the facts to me about when she was a little girl and my mother had taken apart an old yellow dress that had come in a bag from Pennsylvania. She opened out the fullness of the skirt, washed and ironed the fabric and used the yards of material to make her a beautiful garment.

It was typical in those days in the early 1950s, for people in Cape Breton to receive used clothing from the 'Boston States' where more fortunate people lived. That was the beginning of my understanding about the complexities of 'difference', of social class and status, where one group of people accepts the leftovers from another group and makes necessary and useful items. The need for survival had prompted and sharpened one group's adeptness and creativity, while the wealthy bought what they wanted and discarded it as the styles changed.

It was a time in history when my island people were forced to be frugal and had to judge an item to be 'practical' and 'serviceable' before a purchase was made. It appeared to me that some people were luckier and could buy things on a whim, then scrap them when they grew tired of them. Thank God I never had the luxury of such wastefulness.

The woman smiled and smiled at me as she spoke about 'that yellow dress' and about a time in her life when, as one of many children, she did not feel particularly unique. Years later she could still proudly tell me, *"Annie Margaret took the time to listen to me and to make that yellow dress for me."* Over fifty years later, my mother's efforts to instill confidence in her, through a yellow dress with a square neckline and a bow on the back, still remains a pivotal reminder of a time when she felt very special indeed.

These women set the example for me with their respect for the needs of others. No request was too preposterous. As a child, I often watched my mother prepare and handle fabrics as a means of healing herself from her many hurts. Such a close relationship with her fabrics, smelling the wool, touching the weaving, holding, matching and cutting cloth must indeed have held healing properties that gave her mastery in that one area of her life.

These women had foresight, thrift, creativity and wisdom. Although not formally educated, they were truly wise women. Compensating for husbands' low incomes while raising a family under difficult circumstances, their work was invisible for the most part and remains unrecorded until now. Like so many pioneer women whose caring work made necessary and positive contributions throughout history, they were wonderful, resourceful and talented women.

As their heir, my home naturally seemed to be the place to get things fixed and have a good cup of tea. I didn't drive, so people brought their work to be done amid the rising bread to be baked, the laundry that was an ever-growing heap, and my six children who ran about my feet.

Even in my protests, people continued to come because they believed they could trust my work. After all, I was Annie Margaret's daughter, who had learned to sew from Ellen Doyle. I worked hard not to disappoint these people and to carry on the good name of my ancestors. In time, I became a well-respected seamstress in Mabou, and many people brought their problems to my table.

My sewing machine was always on the kitchen table, fabric from some project scattered about, sometimes with the cat asleep in the midst of some-one's expensive material. I never intended to live my life that way. But for well over 40 years, I used my inherent skills to provide a service for others, doing what my ancestors had done. Even though I believed that I couldn't live up to their great skills, other people believed that I could. People had belief in me. Their faith was my encouragement to meet their needs.

And so I became a self-taught seamstress. In addition to making every possible novelty that I could think of for my children, I worked for people to make dresses, gowns, dolls, drapes, kilts and church banners. I clothed all the female members of multiple wedding parties, including the bride. Then I used the leftover scraps to make quilts for my own children. I sewed every-thing for everyone, from Girl Guide badge to the ribbons of veterans' medals. I sewed for the members of the Rankin Family and for Natalie MacMaster, before they were famous. My entire maied life was spent working out of my kitchen, for people who believed I could make or fix anything because, "...*it's in your people.*"

As I grew more comfortable with people, they started to confide in me about their relationships, their marriages and children, in-laws, religious issues and community conflicts. They told me it felt good to talk to me. What I did not know was that, in addition to being a seamstress, I was actu-ally doing social work, taking it out of the office and conducting it in a dif-ferent environment—my kitchen—something today that carries the fancy term 'eco-therapy'.

A diverse range of people came with a diverse range of chores for me to do. They expressed quite bluntly, *"Donelda, you can fix this?"* stating, asking, and telling me all in the same intonation. Young and old men came to me with their green work pants and coveralls to be hemmed, children brought their toys, newly-engaged women came in hopes that I would make their wedding gowns. Frantic and seething mothers begged to have their child's 4-H projects finished—just under the wire before Exhibition Day! Teenagers brought elaborate and expensive dreams of the ultimate prom dress, while moms relied on me to prevail on the side of reality and common sense.

Some people brought work to me that another had attempted to fix but had only made the problem worse.

Some people brought aged and yellowed wedding gowns to be cut down into christening gowns. I once made a pair of pajamas for a man so large, he couldn't purchase properly fitted clothing. And when a friend had her breast removed, I filled one side of her bra with stuffing and weighted it down with sand. Another woman needed two shoulder pads on one shoulder of her blouses. She had a spinal condition that caused one shoulder to be lower. More time was spent fixing the problem than discussing how the injury occurred.

There were times when I had to put Velcro tabs on shirts so that physically challenged people could proudly dress themselves. Several groups of women were difficult to fit consistently, as their sizes kept changing. One group was anorexic and the others were pregnant brides-to-be. And sometimes I had to gently insinuate that perhaps the style, fabric or design that a person had chosen might not be the most flattering for their present shape. I would coyly suggest, *"Have you ever thought of wearing it this way?"* I had to remember to respect people when their decision was to go forward with their original idea, despite what I thought was an awkward fit.

My customers, who became more plentiful over the years, had a wide range of personalities. I met so many wonderful people in my many years as a seamstress. I can also say I am glad I owned the privilege of refusing to work for the not-so-nice people. Not every job has that luxury. My customers brought a wide range of interesting issues to my table. Sometimes they came because they had ruined another person's garment and were frantic to restore it. Cigarette burns were common. Once I worked for a grieving relative, preparing a tiny dress for a new baby to be buried in. People came because they had out-grown their favourite garment but wanted to salvage what they could for someone special. At times, a family would want their deceased child's clothing made into a quilt. That is very emotional work.

Probably the most resistant customers were those women chosen as bridesmaids. Besides being resentful about paying for yards of burgundy, peach or purple satin material (with matching stilettos) they minded paying the price of seamstress work for puffy sleeved, Cinderella-styled gowns with huge trailing bows on the backsides. No matter how well I did my work, or how well the gowns fit, there was no way to make these gals feel good about being forced to wear those awful creations. They simply didn't want to be wearing them at all.

Most of my customers were women. Some had no inhibitions about stripping down and getting into their new outfits, but others were much more modest. In their various stages of undress, I was privy to women's scars, those of multiple Caesarian births, stretch marks from pregnancies, and evidence of gall bladder operations, hysterectomies, mastectomies, and colostomies. One woman had a rare disorder that rendered her left leg five times the size of the other one. Hence, she had to have her clothing custom made. One time, I made the wrong leg as the bigger one. After realizing and admitting my mistake to her, we had a good laugh together and decided to start again. To be part of such human suffering was always very humbling for me. To be granted the chance to start again is always a redemptive and face-saving experience.

I often came to the rescue for my good friend whose sewing abilities were limited to taping the hem of her slacks with gray duct tape. I firmly believe she took sewing lessons from Ava Gabor on *Green Acres*, who darned her husband's woolen socks by stapling the holes closed. I had one male customer whose children goaded me into playing tricks on their father. Without fail, I would sew his pockets closed and zippers open and make one leg shorter than the other. At times I would sew huge colourful patches on the rear-end. This work was tediously done on purpose by me, just for the delight of his kids. The work was a complete nuisance to him if he picked up his garments minutes before he needed to wear them. To undo my devilry was less work for him than it was for me to arrange—but that didn't matter to me. I was always good for the extra work at his expense, and for the excitement of his kids—and he always came back for more.

After many years of sewing, I thought it would be cool to have my own symbol to autograph my creations. I decided on the Cape Breton tartan, shaped into a heart. So I put two-way carpet tape on the back of the tartan, cut out a fat heart and peeled the paper off the other side so I could adhere it onto my creations. It was and is still a hit, always placed in the lower right-hand corner of my quilts. It pleases me greatly when people excitedly ask…*"where's the heart, where's the heart?"*

I learned a lot of what I needed to know about life from weaving in and ironing out the wrinkles of the fabric of these people's lives—but when my mother took apart her own winter coat to make a coat for me, I learned everything I ever needed to know about becoming a social worker.

My mother knew I had no winter coat and that I was cold. She assessed the situation, calculated her resources and looked at the pros and cons of each choice and at the consequences of each decision. Finally, with few resources, but with much practicality, inner confidence and sacrifice, she decided to take her own coat apart and make it again to fit me. It was teal blue, had deep pockets, made of warm Melton cloth, the inside made warm with satin lining, and it closed with huge buttons.

As a child, I certainly did not appreciate this act of love as I do now, nor did I realize how her actions would inspire my own life. I now believe that everything I ever needed to know about social work came from her motivation to take apart and remake that teal blue coat for me.

My mother and grandmother would certainly have laughed to have their sewing work compared to social work—if they even knew what social work was. However, their philosophies for helping people were very much those of the social work profession. They made changes in the best interests of their children and for the local people. They planned and researched the topic of sewing until they felt comfortable offering advice to others.

Like social workers, they got to know their customers, the people who owned the basis of the solution and who simply required the services of a skilled person to put the pieces back together again. My ancestors respected and believed in the worth of local folk and the materials they brought to the table. They were competent people who had a high standard of excellence as they worked directly with people. Some customers were more unfortunate while some were disabled, some were wealthy but without even a thimble of common sense, while others were excellent sharp-witted people but with no money.

My women relatives volunteered advice, and researched their planning strategies with practical insight and ability, to ensure the least restrictive 'fit' that would provide personal fulfillment. Brainstorming with the customer was necessary for self-determination, decision-making and the meeting of one's needs. Like my grandmother's customers did for her and like I did for my mother, the client must go get the material and look around their lives to gather up their issues, to bring to the table. Then a therapist will sit with them and help them put things back together again, albeit in a different form this time. Together, a comfortable fit can be found. If we do not know how to do something, we can say, *"I don't know how to do this, but I sure will find out."*

Like social workers, my people advocated for change in the best interests of people while protecting personal facts about individual flaws and scars. As well, I believe I have never exploited these important relationships and did protect the naked truth about many people. Collectively, we gave people hope. My mother, grandmother and I used our abilities to make a difference in people's lives. Without adequate means to provide everything ourselves, we asked others to assist us, by doing their part. When my mother needed additional help, a referral was made to the T. Eaton Company. Hence, the fit of my new coat became tailor-made just for me.

The benefits of that fit have lasted a lifetime for me and I unfold new benefits every day. The coat was comfortable, serviceable, and was the least cost to the provider and consumer, in this case, a child—and it lasted two whole winters. It has taken me this long in life to understand why the making of that coat, my culture, my history, my people, and my traditions have fit so well into my life. I have come to fully realize that indeed! I now fit very well with them. My sewing basket of notions is filled with the instructions passed to me by my people.

When clients come to social workers, the goal will be to find a fit that is highly individualized. Some people will suffer from Alzheimer's disease. Their needs will differ from others with the same disease. Several may need special help in some areas while others will not need the same help in the same area. Some clients will come willingly, and others not, because they will be mandated clients, with top-down recommendations like the bridesmaids had. They will hate the fit and begrudge the fact that they have to attend. No matter how well we do our work, these people will **not** be happy with the 'fit', because they simply do not want to be there.

People will come to us with their disabilities, like the woman who had a missing breast, or because they cannot fit the standardized labelling that they have to fit into, for others' agendas. Others will come because they need help having closure and need that little piece of Velcro or perhaps another shoulder pad to even up their position. They may need help grieving because they had to bury a child, or unexpectedly prepare for a wedding or a wake, or are older citizens who need a quieter, slower approach. People will come to us because they have damaged another person or their reputation, and will need help to restore it and find self-forgiveness in the process. Others will come to us because their situations keep changing, due to eating disorders, divorce, alcoholism or pregnancies. People may come to us damaged by another worker's advice or attitudes.

Our work will **not** be limited to daylight hours. I used to stay up late at night to sew, to think and to visually rotate fabrics in my mind to be able to cut the material in the most practical way. Then, I would arise early the next morning to do the work while my children were still sleeping. One morning I got up early to finish a wedding gown. In order to see the neckline on the dress, I put it on myself. It was around 5 a.m. when someone suddenly arrived at the door hoping my husband would be up. I was standing in the middle of the kitchen with someone's white flowing bridal gown on, sizing it in the mirror that was leaning against the wall. He stared at me and stared at the dress. Before I could explain, he hurriedly departed, stating, *"No, it's ok, don't explain. I don't need to know".* There I was in peals of laughter. Our social work will take place when it must, and we may not always be able to explain our actions to others.

Notions in my basket of instructions include pieces of advice for me to follow. Never underestimate the power of someone's trust in you. Push yourself beyond their expectations to meet the goal. Let others tell you that you are doing okay—part of doing a good job is hearing others say it. One of the seven deadly sins we take seriously in Cape Breton is that to boast is a terrible thing—so let others tell you if you are doing a good job.

There will be a logical sequence of orders to follow in our workplaces but we can improvise sometimes and change the pattern a bit. Spend as little time as possible on how the damage happened; focus instead on how to resolve the issue. Visualize the many possibilities of people before you even get to know their texture. Be careful to guide the client with appropriate advice. Sew for people you like, but never, ever use your social work training and experience on family.

People will always be like the fabrics they bring to be sewn, some will be sturdy, some transparent, some falling apart while others will be rough, tattered or with their 'nap' pushed in the wrong direction. There will always be those people, like the special swatches of material that I keep. Those are the pieces that little can be done with, so they are kept in a special place in my trunk of material, and are simply loved by me.

Some people will be very conservative in revealing their secrets while others will quickly bare everything, sometimes without the expected emotions that might accompany such pain. Some will look pretty sturdy on the outside only to reveal that they are in need of some real patching up. Others will look pretty tattered but really have very strong interfacing. Sometimes the social worker will hurt, cry and bleed for the situation just as a seamstress hurts when she pricks her finger with the needle while doing her fancy work.

Fabric can represent therapists as well as clients. Some will be soft, tough, transparent or perhaps not sturdy enough. I have seen those who are rough, dirty, and tough as leather, slippery, tattered and coming apart at the seams like cheesecloth themselves. I have also known those who are solid but flexible, soft and reliable, serviceable weather-resistant therapists. It is important to remember there is a wide selection to choose from. Use wisdom when tempted by a bargain.

Sometimes we may have to have to place a referral for special alterations, like when my mother ordered a fur collar from a catalogue. Sometimes, for various reasons, as I did, we may all have to wait a bit for the project to be finished. Calamities happen and then we move on.

The measuring tape of my *Instruction Manual* tells me to respect those people who are stripped down to nearly nothing in their shame and hurt. Sometimes all we can do is hold them in our 'special place' and hope for the best, in a plan we don't understand. It will be necessary to remember to remind our clients that not everyone will like the 'fit' they have chosen for themselves, as with separation, adoption and divorce. I hope I remember to celebrate even small successes with special little pieces of trim. And to remember that there is a lot we can do to fix ourselves, by heeding our own suggestion of, *"...have I ever thought of doing it this way?"*

One time, a woman who had heard about my fascination with making dolls, called me from somewhere. She wanted a special order. It would be a gift to herself, from herself, to be made specifically for herself to meet an unfulfilled child-hood wish. It was also going to serve several other needs too. She wanted it to be a large doll with blond curly hair and wearing a beautiful christen-ing gown. She also did not want to see the finished product at any point prior to completion—she wanted me to wrap it in nice wrapping paper and then send it to her, near a certain date, sent from herself. Well, I was really into people recognizing their needs and fulfilling them in any way they could. I recognized the emotional work she was doing, just from the description of the order. I assured her I would do it well and send it to the General Delivery address she provided me. She sent a cheque in the mail and I sent her the doll, made to order, beautiful, and wrapped as prettily as any gift would be for someone special. I received a card from her later. She expressed her delight at having received from me and herself, what she always wanted from someone else. The christening gown—made from the most beautiful material I could find, complete with lovely ribbons and lace, was more than she ever expected to receive, but it was exactly what she wanted. Perhaps it coincided with a renewal of faith.

I felt I had cooperated in her healing process and was delighted to do so. I still have the picture that I took of the doll before I sent it to her. I know, somewhere, it is still held in high esteem by its owner. I am proud of myself for understanding issues like hers, even though at the time, I had no social work training, not even a high school certificate nor a driver's license. I was still doing social work out of my kitchen. Funny, I have never met that woman, nor do I expect to—our contact was all by phone and by mail, not unlike the work that Help Line and Crisis Intervention people do every day.

People will come to get married, to divorce, to cry, to bury someone or to fix something they broke, to make something useful out of an old habit without throwing out all the material. All they need is a private place, someone they trust and license to tell their deepest secrets to a stranger. It is an honour to be the one they tell their private hurts to.

Sometimes that piece of thread, left over in the yellow bowl—useless to most people—is just the right thing for a certain someone. We will help people slowly pull apart the threads that have been keeping their lives together in its present state. Sometimes people will already be coming apart at the seams and need some tightening in places. Sometimes a person can feel special from having a used item from a grab bag, especially when it is tailored to fit only them. Sometimes we have to forgive our own mistakes and start all over again. Sometimes a piece of duct tape can be a temporary fix until there is time for the real work to be done. Larger pieces of the fabric of people's lives will gently be placed on the table so they can be cut down again, re-measured, viewed from a different perspective and made into a more serviceable fit. Smaller pieces can always be saved to fix when there is more time. Sometimes it's their time to throw out those old habits.

The reputation of the worker is very important. My mother naturally came into her skills from her mother, but created her own respected reputation. Consequently, I inherited from both women. Hopefully, I've achieved the same fine reputation.

Nevertheless, excellence is not something that we tell others we have, it's a characteristic recognized by others that hopefully will be spoken of for generations. Strive to be spoken of with respect. Workers and agencies will need to strive for that excellence, to match clients and solutions properly, to do the finer needlework themselves to assure quality control, and to try not to rub the nap the wrong way. We must pardon ourselves when we do, because it is nearly impossible **not** to rub someone the wrong way somewhere along this journey.

Social work practice, like sewing, is hard to do, but fun, rewarding, productive and requires a stubborn but knowledgeable touch. We need courage when dealing with the many different, wonderful and miserable people we encounter along the way.

But, we can't sew for others if we can't sew at all. I firmly believe we all own the responsibility to examine and to pull apart every thread of our own lives, to check for flaws in the weaving, to find the torn areas, and to seek ways to patch them up. What I believe is integral to the mental health of the social worker, is that we must know those weaker areas in the texture of our lives and what types of exposure can stress them. Perhaps we need a little sign on our chest stating, *"Do not place in hot water"*. We have to be aware of where we can get hurt and then take care to protect ourselves in those areas.

Today, the tools of the sewing trade are still the same—sturdy scissors, measuring tapes, sewing machines, pins, needles and buttons among all the other miscellaneous threads. With these, many alterations can be made; things can be improved or improvised like an old coat, adjusted for another fit. In like manner, empathy, kindness, listening skills and respect do not go out of style for the seamstress, the therapist or the social worker. My manual says remember not to charge forward for the bargains that modernity offers but to remember those little old-fashioned treatments that still have some function for many people. My manual also says have faith. Faith in God, in myself and faith in the client. They are the ones who know what is best for them. Help them find that path.

Remember to have a little fun when helping others. Maybe having one pant leg shorter than the other will keep people smiling during a busy day. Remember to have a supply of those big colourful patches because you just never know when you might have to cover your own ass! Keep a little yellow bowl of used items and grab bags nearby so that certain people get their own perfect fit when conventional items do not match. Among the many notions in my manual is my belief that the goal of the therapeutic setting, like the work of the seamstress, is to meet people where they are, work with what they have brought already, maintain their strengths, compensate for their weaknesses and like my mother did for me, to protect the vulnerable child from the cold. In doing so, clients will become empowered and more comfortable when wearing their own choices.

I have spent a lot of time at the sewing machine helping repair the problems of others, but I have also sat in the client's chair, like cheesecloth falling apart, begging someone to show me what a better fit might look like for me. I have found that, for all my flaws, there were complementary, stronger strands in my character that have compensated for the rips and tears. Because I did my own emotional work, I have found a better fit for my life, in many ways. I believe we need to seek out new patterns to decorate our own lives. If we maintain the stronger skeins and seek to strengthen the weaker ones, we can be the same example of excellence that my female ancestors were for me.

In May of 2001 I walked, tired and proud across the stage at St. Francis Xavier University to receive my Bachelor of Arts degree. I had been sewing my own broken life together and doing some of the finer embroidery work that day.

When it was my turn to get my graduation certificate, I placed my right foot on the bottom step of the wooden staircase. I raised my left hand to touch the little white fur band on my blue graduation cape. My experienced fingers, sensitive to the weave in fabrics, instinctively felt the direction of the nap. It was going in the right direction.

I felt as good then as I did on Back Street in 1963. I had made a better 'fit' for my life and I was heading in the right direction.

Two years later, in October of 2003, I would graduate from Dalhousie University with a Bachelor of Social Work. Then my own durability would be tested to see how 'serviceable' I would be in the social work field and what I could bring to the table.

I worked for one year with the Canadian Paraplegic Association after graduation. Then, several part time jobs. I went to Churchill, Manitoba for two years, then Rankin Inlet, Nunavut for two more, working for the Federal Government. I worked hard and saved my money so I could return to my beautiful Cape Breton and buy my own house. And that's exactly what I did.

What will *you* bring to the table?

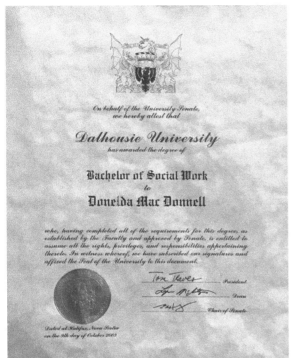

CDY LITTLE FUR COLLAR

My mother was innovative; she had to be. There were few luxuries to make my mother's life easy. She graciously accepted this fact and was very creative in her ability to give her family what she could not buy. I appreciate all she did and I know I never told her. My family lived on 'Back Street' in Mabou, Cape Breton—known officially as Highland Street, where every home had between 5 and 13 children, many of them as poor as we were.

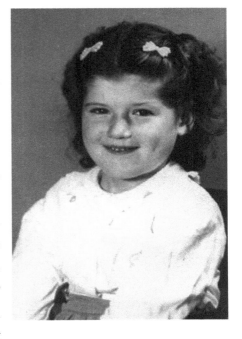

We were a family of eight children plus two parents; three girls and five boys. Several families had a dozen children. It was not unusual for 50 kids to pour out into the short street each morning. Kids biking, skipping, fighting, climbing trees and playing hopscotch were everywhere.

Used coats and boots were passed around from family to family, child to child. Many relatives had left Canada to work in Boston where the multi-talented girls were high in demand. They could cook, clean, bake, sew and take care of children. Better economically situated, many Bostonian families didn't recycle their used items at home; therefore bulging suitcases were sent from the 'Boston States' for us. Once they arrived in Mabou, the perfectly good clothes were jealously fought over; the older and stronger kids always getting the best stuff.

Life was so different in those days. It was during a time when children always went outside on winter mornings and stayed out all day. We were concerned that if we came back into the house to change out of our wet clothes, we would have to stay in. We did not have snowsuits but wore layers and layers of pants and sweaters to keep us warm on the hills behind our house in Mabou. There were no modern technologies. I could hold my pee for a record amount of time. Then our mother would call us in, because she had made a big supper with lots of home-made dishes. While we were playing all day, she had been working.

Aside from the regular condiments such as home-made mustard pickles and green tomato chow-chow, there would always be fresh bread and biscuits

with stew and dumplings or a roast dinner with thick gravy. My favourite dish of all was my mother's pumpkin preserves, made with whole cloves in thick, sweet, syrup. She would sit at the kitchen table and cut the perfectly shaped squares of pumpkin to make the pretty orangey preserves, dotted with little brown cloves. There were no appliances to conveniently cut the peeled slices of pumpkin into the tiny squares, just a sharp knife, a cutting board and lots of patience. When the bottles were filled and the covers were cooling to pop, she would put them on the windowsills and admire her own handiwork. Today, there are kitchen appliances to chop up and mince the woody pulp to make the same dessert. I loved the taste of them. They still remind me of her sitting there and of her labour of love.

My mother often sat in the rocking chair by the kitchen stove holding her babies and singing little Gaelic songs. Four babies were born in rapid succession after my parents married and this took its toll on my mother's health. She would have four more as well. Life was not easy.

But, she was determined to give these babies everything they needed. She would take apart used clothing to be recycled for myself or for one of my siblings. My sisters and brothers sit with me on the red and grey tiled floor covered with newspapers. The floor is freshly scrubbed and polished. That flooring was later changed. On the warming oven of the old Enterprise stove are apple pies and freshly-baked brown raisin bread, the sweet aroma

filling the room. The atmosphere deliciously becomes real to me again as I write this description.

Hanging on the door casings are several little dresses that she made for my little sister, Anita. One dress is mauve and yellow and the other is red velvet with a large white collar. My mother looks sad as she talks to herself and I always try to get near enough to her to hear who she is scolding!

Clyde Nunn's soothing voice comes over CJFX on the old fashioned radio on the little shelf behind the stove. He is reminding the mothers to be sure to put a little more water on the potatoes, which he pronounces 'pid-daid-as.' His deep reassuring voice is always timely as my mother goes to check the steaming vegetables and indeed, she agrees, they have nearly dried up!

I can still remember when it was my turn to have a new Sunday coat. The year is 1963 and I am 11. The skill my mother used to re-craft her own Melton woolen coat was magical to me. First, she opened up the seams and separated all the sections until it looked like a pattern again. Next, she reversed each piece of the material, then cut them all a bit smaller. And finally, she sewed the pieces together again so it became a miniature version of her adult coat, but less a collar.

My mother thinks hard as she sits with her coat on her lap. There will be a logical sequence to the order in which she takes apart and remakes the same project. She opens up the seams and sorts the pieces of material that recently were her coat. Once detached, the sleeves are placed on one side of her chair, buttons are saved in a yellow plastic bowl with the 'hooks and eyes' and strands of thread are wound onto a little piece of cardboard. The thread will be saved in a small tin can—inside a yellow plastic bowl and used later for hand stitching. As the threads holding the coat together are slowly pulled away, the satin lining is removed too. Lint and dust (connichans) fall from the time-pressed seams and are swept away.

Smaller pieces of fabric are saved for making quilts. Larger pieces of material are folded and saved in boxes near her mother's foot-operated Singer sewing machine. These pieces will be used for repairing the knees of my brother's leggings. Little goes into the garbage. The pieces of fabric to be used for my coat are carefully placed on the kitchen table so they can be observed, re-measured, cut down again, viewed in a different way and then re-assembled to make a more serviceable item.

My mother had the inherent gift and skill to mentally and visually rotate each piece of pattern in her mind, before actually cutting fabric, so that the 'right' sides of the material properly faced each other. Like the fur on a cat, the 'nap' of material has to slant in the same direction or the difference will be visible, even from a distance (and other stitchers might 'tsk-tsk-tsk' to one another about the 'poor quality of her work'). My mother was very particular in her sewing methods. When she sewed, the current of the nap never flowed in the wrong direction. Additionally, she would wisely reverse each piece of material to hide the wear spots, creating the perception of a new garment.

She pinned and basted pieces together for my dress rehearsal. Standing high in the centre of the kitchen table and getting weak from the strange height, I modeled my mother's creation for her. She directed me *"turn—a little more—to the other side now—ok—turn around this way."* Then she took another look at how well the coat fit me. Sometimes she took a tuck in here, a dart in there or trimmed a tad off the hem or sleeves. Then, like an artist, she stood back and admired her own handiwork. She decided, with me, if it was a comfortable fit and most importantly, if it was serviceable enough to last another winter.

Then my mother sat at her mother's sewing machine. She sewed the pieces back together again and created the same coat, only smaller. She had found a practical solution that was now a good fit for me. Then she decided that it needed a little embellishment, an elegant touch to celebrate our success. It would need a little fur collar. The recycled thread in the yellow bowl would then be used to sew the collar, the hem and the buttons onto my 'new' coat.

Together my mother and I looked through the forbidden pages of the T. Eaton's catalogue. Well—'eenie-meenie-minie-mowed' over which little fur collar would I be privileged enough to have on my new coat. My mother was careful to guide me in a size and an appropriate price, as it could not exceed the 'Baby Bonus' amount that was allotted to me for one month.

I remember the joyous anticipation I experienced while awaiting that C.O.D. parcel to come into the post office on 'Front Street' in Mabou and the calamity that caused a delay before it could be attached. It came inside a little plastic bag, stapled and then wrapped in brown paper, with my mother's name on it. It had the familiar blue paper on the front signifying the company.

It had come from Eaton's store, all the way from Halifax, which seemed so far away to me then. The collar was very white and quite fluffy although it was short fur. (I hoped it was not a real bunny at one time, but that thought faded as it became closer to being on my coat.) My mother squinted to thread the needle and asked me to help. Her eyes were weaker then and she needed help, as she was not a well woman, but never stopped being a very hard working mother. She would often say, *"If you'll just do the walking, I'll do the rest."*

So I would go around the house to get whatever items she needed and she would sit and do the work. I was close by, recording her every move. It was she who taught me a lesson that I live by to this day, and that is, if I am going to do something, I do it well or I don't do it at all!

So my mother sewed the precious little fur collar on my new teal wool coat. The collar had pure white satin underlining and a little elastic loop to slip over the cloth-covered button. My new winter coat with the little fur collar was finished. I was thrilled. Everyone said, *"I suppose your mother made your coat?"*

I experienced such pride as I walked through the troops of more than 50 children on Back Street. I had on my new coat with the little white fur collar softly touching on my chin. My mother had made it for me. My siblings walked beside me, all wearing their own new coats. I wonder now; did she know how excited I was? Did I tell her, or, like children do, just smile and smile? The richness of that gorgeous colour still brings a warm feeling over me and continues to be my favourite colour today.

I do not have the coat anymore nor do I have my mother. She was a great cook and a self-taught seamstress but she was a hero to her children in many other ways. Today I feel her presence when I wrap up in my teal-coloured blanket or eat some pumpkin preserves. I learned to sew and I cook, but I could never match the quality of her preserves. Recently my little daughter threaded a needle for me, because I was squinting to do it myself. I was making something for her, just like my mother had done for me.

Eaton's seemed to be so far away to me then and it really wasn't. Winters seemed to be more fun then, but they really weren't, I suppose. I just don't go out and stay there all day in wet clothes! The little fur collar seemed to be the most expensive item in the world but it wasn't. My mother's pumpkin preservers seemed to be the best tasting dish I ever ate. But my mother seemed to be the hardest working mother in the world and that I'm really sure of.

I do not recall my mother ever having another new coat. Later in her life, she became very ill and subsequently died when I was 20 years old, leaving young children to mourn her loss. I wish my kids had known her. Today as an adult and as a mother myself, I wonder if she went without a coat so that I would have one? I do all the same things myself now; I save buttons, I cut away second-hand clothes to make new items and I sacrifice for my children. I am very innovative, I have to be. There have been few luxuries. I have my mother to thank for teaching me how to be able to survive.

ƑATHER'S MORNING RITUAL

When I was a very little girl, I loved to be around my father. To me he was a huge man who always smelled of balsam, sweat, Export cigarette 'makins' and Old Spice after-shave lotion. His name was Donald but he was Daddy to me. After work, he sat in the wooden rocking chair beside the wood stove, and I would wiggle into his arms. Resting his elbows on his knees, he would put his big hands together and interlock his fingers to make a swing for me. I would sway back and forth, sometimes burning my hair on his cigarette, and the stink was awful! When he grew weary of the game, he would run his unshaven face on mine. The whisker burn would send me running, but not for long! I was restless and would wiggle my way back into his arms again. *"Swing me, Daddy"* I would beg him again and again. The cycle went on and on.

I was the saucy little kid in the family and won my father's approval by saying whatever he wanted to hear—no matter how outrageous it was—just to make him laugh. Winking at whoever was present, he would set me up to say something that would send everyone into fits of laughter. Then he would say something in Gaelic that I would not understand. I would ask him a hundred times what he had said. My mother, frowning in disap-proval, would try sending me to bed, but I would only march right back downstairs. Only after my father had paid me a dime to bite my big toe, would I go to bed.

I can still see him sitting there, flicking his cigarette ash into the cuff of his pant leg or in his shirt pocket. After he shook the sawdust from his work boots and pant legs onto the floor, I would shape a little pile and play with it. I loved everything about him. He owned pulp trucks and when I wasn't in one, I was on the back of one, or else begging permission to go to the mill in Hawkesbury.

I was so proud of my father. When Remembrance Day came, I would get out the little box that held his medals. The medals were wrapped in a plastic bag inside. I would shine them all with Silvo, so he could sport them in the parade.

I would run to get his Zippo lighter, his cigarettes and his beer for him. I would have done anything for him. When he wasn't around, I would mimic him. After my mother had taken the clothes from the line in the winter, I would dance around the kitchen with his frozen long-johns in my arms. The Stanfield underwear, the size of a full-grown man, would be frozen stiff and flat as a board. If the drawbridge was frozen open, it would be even funnier. Soon they would start to thaw and get soggy, but I would still be dancing with them as they collapsed slowly over my head and shoulders from the heat. After several minutes my dancing partner would be a heap on the floor and my mother would be laughing hysterically. She would get a great kick out of my antics. This pleased me greatly because she was always so tired from her hard work. I loved to hear her laugh. But, the clothes were not taken off the line until bedtime—and not a good time for me to put on a show! The other kids would get caught up in the hilarity and then were harder to settle down.

I loved to imitate my father playing cards. Hollering, *"Skunk!"* or *"60 for 120"*. I would slam my fist on the table with delight the way he would—when he was winning! When the local radio station played fiddle music, I would jump up and step dance just like my uncle, John A. would do. I also loved to imitate my aunts with their big hair and their hearty laughter.

My father was a veteran of the Second World War. Every February he had to go to Camp Hill Hospital in Halifax for tests. While waiting in the hospital, he probably had time to remember that my birthday was that month. At least, I think that's why I would receive a present from my father whenever he returned. In my mind's eye, I can still see the beautiful peach-coloured, plaid dress that he had bought for me once. It was spread out on my bed one morning when I awoke, and I just knew it had come from him. My siblings were jealous and accused me of being spoiled, but I didn't care. I loved that dress and wore it every day until my mother had to take it off me, just to wash it.

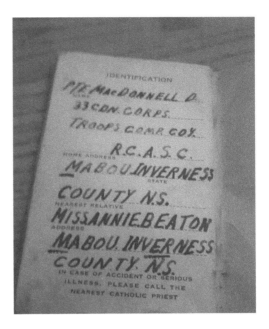

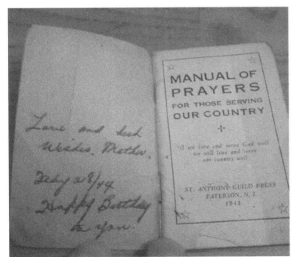

My father's army prayer book and WWII medals

I was a very curious kid. Little went on in our house that I did not know about. I was always aware of my surroundings—where visitors sat, what they wore or how they sounded when they spoke or laughed. I can recall with great clarity how most events evolved.

I remember getting up sometimes just to watch my father 'get the fire going' for the day. I would kneel quietly on the floor and watch him through the iron grate on my bedroom floor. It was right above the kitchen stove. The light in the kitchen was on as it would still be dark outside. The tiled floor was covered with newspapers and my mother's plants were in the tin cans on the windowsills. The wainscoting on the kitchen walls was pale green. My father would have on his long underwear (my dancing partner from the night before) and his work pants over them. The upper part of the underwear was still uncovered, as he hadn't yet donned his plaid shirt. His underwear sleeves were rolled up, and his hair was sticking up on one side.

Although I would be freezing cold, clad only in my pajamas, it was worth the inconvenience just to watch the ensuing ritual. My father was about to light the morning fire. Rooting around the stove, he first made certain that everything was there to get the fire going. Certain attachments are needed to operate a stove, one being a crank: an iron handle. It was affixed to a small post inside the front door, and would open and close the grates located on the inside of the stove. My father would shake this iron handle back and forth, until all the ashes from the day before had fallen into the ash box below, and then the handle was returned behind the stove. Next, he would take the newspapers off the clean floor where my mother had placed them—after scrubbing the night before. Glancing over the papers to see if he had missed any news, my father would then crumple the papers and stuff them on the empty grates inside the stove. The left hand side of the stove top would be lifted up and held open on a small lip—designed just to hold it there. The kindling (thin pieces of wood) was removed from the oven, where they had dried all night. Then they were placed in a criss-cross position on the crumpled newspaper. This would allow the air to flow through them. If any cardboard was handy, it would be added to help kindle the flame. More kindling was added before the cover was put down.

My father would then take the little box of Eddy matches off the warming oven, strike a wooden match on the sulphur side of it and light his cigarette. Other times he would scratch the match inside the hole in the stove covers. Then he would light the fire from the match. When it was burning quite well, he might twist a piece of newspaper, stick it up the open side-draft and light his cigarette that way. I would inhale deeply as the fresh aroma of newly lit tobacco drifted my way.

The damper on the stovepipe was adjusted to allow air to flow into the stove and out again, ventilating and fanning the flames. Another lever on the back of the stove top was used to regulate and groom the fire. He would fan the open side-draft and poke in the stove top a few times to keep things going. The lifter for the stove top covers was a hand-held, circular wire fixture that fit in the little square holes in each cover. Even though some covers were smaller, the handle fit them all. The lifter had to be held in a certain way or else the hot round cover would fall off and hit the floor, leaving a permanent burn mark. Instinctively knowing this, my father held this lifter carefully to add several small, dry pieces of birch on the kindling. Many floors had the tell-tale marks of a hot cover that had fallen and rolled in circles before it set still.

Now fully ignited, the fire would blaze as my father disturbed it from time to time with the poker. He continued to add more wood from the wood box behind the stove until a huge piece would be set in the red coals to last for some time. It would make a solid foundation to hold a shovelful of coal that would be scooped from the scuttle with the little coal shovel. Only then, having stoked the fire well, did my father begin the process of making his morning tea and of getting dressed. The kettle would be emptied, then filled again and perhaps some 'grounds' would fall out. Then it was placed in the middle of the stove to catch the most heat.

Sitting in the rocking chair beside the stove Daddy would swing his left leg onto his other knee to put one sock on his foot. Then, placing that left foot on the floor with a thump; he would pull the sock up almost to his knee; then roll it back down again, until it looked like a donut around his ankle. Pleating the bottom of his long underwear at his ankle, he would unroll the donut sock over it and there it stayed all day. My father once told me he had learned this routine in the army where spats were worn over the sock and pant leg. But since he was no longer in the army, his work boot would be laced around the ankle for the same effect.

The green work-pant leg would be let down over the sock and long under-wear ensemble. The same process was repeated with another woolen sock that had been knit by my mother. This sock was worn over the pants and folded down a bit in winter. A little of the tight pant leg would be pulled up from the sock, to allow for some slack. Later on, his boots—warming on the open oven door—were pulled on over both pairs of the thick homemade socks. The lacing of the boots had to be perfect—enough lace would be left to go around the ankle twice and finally tied in the front, a little to the inside of the ankle. This routine—two socks on each foot, pant legs over the pleated underwear, then boots over socks—was done with great precision every day.

By this time, the kettle would be sizzling happily and the room would be bursting with the heat. When the room became quite hot, my father would begin to open, one at a time, the doors that led into the rest of the house. At this point, I would get up from my position over the grate and move over to the stairway where I could watch my father from a different angle. Avoiding certain steps that were known to creak, I crouched on the stairway. Peering out between the rungs under the banister, I just watched and mentally recorded all that I saw. The heat from the stove, now flowing from the kitchen into the hallway and up the stairs, made me feel a little warmer. The sound of the local radio station, CJFX, drifted into the upstairs rooms with the smell of fresh tea and cigarette smoke.

Finally, the stove was lit, the room was warm, tea was on, and the ritual of socks over the underwear and more socks over the pants legs was over. The heat rising from the stove was visible, making the air wobbly and distorting everything behind it. Now, from my perch, I knew the next move very well. My father would take his old rosary beads off the nail beside the hall door. Turning off the radio, he would kneel down at the rocking chair, facing the Sacred Heart picture above the door. Then he would bless himself, place his face in his hands and begin to say his morning prayers. I had to be really quiet now because there were no other sounds to conceal my presence. I would listen to him sighing heavily, as his prayers drifted toward Heaven and toward me. From time to time, he would often shift his position to look at the beads, to see what decade he was on, then continue with a sigh as he prayed in Gaelic.

My father thought he was alone. If he had ever looked up and seen me there, I think I would have scared him half to death. But I was just a little girl, sitting there, admiring the man whose name I had been given and whom I loved so much. But I kept my distance, and never joined him. My time with him would come when he returned from work and then swing me in his arms. Many times I witnessed this ritual in awe where the warm atmosphere of the stove and smell of the fire enhanced the scene.

It is a powerful moment for a child to see her parent in prayer, and I have never forgotten the sight of my father, kneeling beside the kitchen stove. I was accustomed to seeing my mother in prayer, as the Holy Rosary was her constant companion. But for my father, this was supposed to be a private gesture between himself and his Maker. Except that this sacred moment was not private. I was there and I've never forgotten it.

Prayers said, the fire sending waves of heat throughout the house, my father now poured his tea into a cup and then into a saucer. He held the saucer in front of him, with his thumbs and middle fingers under the sides of the saucer and his forefingers on the top of it. One finger was slightly disfigured where it had once been deeply cut. The steaming tea would cool as he blew over it, making little ripples in the pool of liquid in the saucer. Then, putting his lips to the edge of the saucer, he would slurp it noisily, enjoying the full effect of 'a good cup of tea'. Each drink of tea was taken in this fashion.

Having had this hour to prepare himself for the day, my father would now sit beside the stove, poking the fire from time to time, thinking his thoughts. As for me, I would steal away to my room and wait for him to let out a roar for everyone to get up. This would be my moment to magically appear as if I had just gotten up. When I arrived in the kitchen, my father (who was by now playing solitaire) would ask me to make him a cup of tea. Scottish people can never get enough tea so this was not an unusual request. My mother would then appear and wrap an apron around her swollen waist. Simultaneously, she would place the cast iron frying pan on the stove with a pot of water to boil for porridge. A pinch of salt was added. Daddy would have bacon and eggs for breakfast. The aroma of toast cooking over the hot coals in the stove, along with the sound of popping and sizzling bacon, would fill the kitchen. The radio announcer was calling for snow. One by one my siblings would make their way down the stairs, and my mother would dish out the porridge. With brown sugar and milk, it made a perfect breakfast. Before long, my brothers and sisters and I would be fighting over who would get the biggest bowl of porridge. That was when my father would get up from the table and go to work. Whatever porridge was left over would go in the bread she would make, including what was left in the bowls. Milk and brown sugar included. She made the best bread.

My father's morning ritual was just a small part of his day, but it was very comforting to me. It recurred with regularity and remained constant throughout my childhood in the 1950s and '60s, except, when he would go 'away' to work, then my mother would perform the same procedures.

Nothing stayed the same. Everything changed over time and my father did too. The drink often got the best of him. Waiting for him to go on a tear or go on a pledge was awfully hard on everyone. I lost my connection with him and never got it back.

I have long since moved from that house and am nearly a half a century in age (at the time of this writing). My mother passed away many years ago and my father is 80 years old (my father has since died). I am a parent myself. Wood stoves, for the most part, have been replaced by modern electric heat. Still, I could make a fire in my sleep if I had to. Every time I see a pulp truck go by, I inhale and relive my childhood love of them. A lot of things have changed, but the image of my father praying in the warmth of the morning fire is still a real and special memory to me.

bEAD OF SILVER bAIR

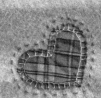

Leaning on her door frame,
I stand silent to have a look,
At the lady worn and wrinkled
Like a well-used favourite book.

In her flowered dress and woolen sweater,
M'lady's lost in thought,
With stockings twisted 'n' gaudy brooch
She rocks beside her cot.

Slowly I approach her,
Studying time upon her face.
Still fleshy but with age spots,
From years at a hectic pace.

I wonder who she thinks of
In her head of silver hair
With a choice of near ten decades
As time stands still in there.

Is it her Irish heritage?
She can recall so clear
How her parents often spoke of
Walter the Pioneer?

Who sailed from Wexford, Ireland
In eighteen hundred fifteen;
An Irish couple with four children
Walter Moran and Mary Breen.

They landed in Cape Breton
River Centre looked like home
It reminded them of Ireland
So they didn't feel forlorn.

Their son John took an Irish wife
Elizabeth Murphy was his bride
They received a Grant of Land
Thirteen children were their pride.

A son, Daniel wed Jessie O'Connor
And repeated his father's life
Another baker's dozen.
He took an Irish wife.

The oldest was Mary Ellen
Who now rocks beside her bed.
It is her I wonder about
And the life that she has led.

Is it her busy childhood
Of life in green Glencoe?
The eldest of thirteen children
Nearly one hundred years ago?

Or memories when the bridge was built
That she crossed to go to school?
How she loved to take her lunch pail
And her little slate and rule!

The dark-eyed Irish lass
Was churning, weaving, praying
Running in clovered meadows
Gathering eggs hens were laying.

She learned early how to work
With her mother Jessie and her father Dan

Thrashing grain in the field
So lived Mary Ellen Moran.

Then it was life in the Margarees
With babies at her breast
Planning to stay there forever
But whoever would have guessed?

Of the dream she had foreseen
Her husband's death and wake?
How she cried the following day
When he drowned upon the Lake.

The hunger of the Thirties
To a widow wasn't kind.
It forced her to leave Cape Breton
And her two babies behind.

Was it the long train trip to Boston
That she sobbed for every mile?
When the train pulled into the station,
The country girl was out of style.

Now Mary Ellen MacFarlane
Suffering with her grief,
Had to find employment
Hoping time there would be brief.

A doctor's nurse-maid she would be
In uniform and cap
She earned the title Cook!
They obeyed her with a snap!

Was it catering those lavish parties?
With champagne and chandeliers
And solid silver tableware
To please the doctor's peers?

Since she was so lonesome
She gave her heart to one
And little Martha filled the need
Of her daughter and her son.

In that mansion there were three Mary's
And confusion always reigned
So Martha then decided
That "Molly" would be her name.

For over a quarter century
She worked and danced and grieved
Sending home her meager earnings,
And Molly felt relieved.

Good times and hard times
Passed those years of pain
She worked her way in luxury
And earned herself a name.

Keeping touch with Kay and Alex
(She was still their mother)
But they were only children
Who were fonder of another.

She tried to tie them to her apron
But now they were all grown
In her heart they were still her babies
They were only out on loan.

Both children joined the service
As World War II was on
And then they soon were married
And another generation dawned.

While life forced her to be independent
She re-kindled an old flame
And Molly soon fell in love.
And so became "Mrs. MacLean".

Second marriages for both
Neil doted on his wife.
They were both surprised and happy
When she felt the stir of life.

Now the baby they expected
Drew his first breath and his last
It robbed the spirit in Molly
And her hopes of motherhood crashed.

Homeward finally to Cape Breton
Housekeeping in Port Hood
They started up a business,
As only Molly could.

She called it The Village Tearoom
She was busy as a bee.
Homemade meals and rooms for rent
Fresh apple pies and tea!

I guess I made a noise
And she asked me who was there
I touched her hand and told her
That I had some time to share.

She didn't move her eyes
They had long since ceased to see
But I knew on her expression
That she was happy to see me.

She asked at once of Angus
And I knew again her thoughts
Were of the little black-eyed boy
And the joy that he had brought.

She couldn't remember yesterday
So I took her back in time
To the summer of fifty-three
When she was fifty-nine.

Her brother Hughie's wife had died
Five small children needed homes
And the three that Molly took
Proved too much for weary bones.

So she made a home for Angus
He was the smallest one.
Neil was in his glory
Because now they had their son.

The old man built up the business
With Angus close behind
But Neil's heart stopped one day
When the little boy was nine.

Molly's heart was broken
This blow was very bad

It was another re-adjustment
For the lonesome little lad.

Then a sad twist of fate
Brought some joy to Molly's arms
"Little Mary" came to stay
With all her smiles and charms.

Angus was ecstatic
And devoted to the girl
He'd carry her to and from the beach
With her black and bouncy curls.

Angus passed his boyhood years
They made the house a home
But when he grew to be a man
Molly dined alone.

"This is no place for old people"
She complained about the Home
And I am very grateful
That we are all alone.

Molly needs help with everything
Resenting every minute,
She talked a lot of Heaven
Wishing she was in it.

I yearn at once to hug her
But she is forbidden ground
She had taught us not to touch her
When she was young and sound.

She feels cheated and forgotten
But now I feel the same
She just wants to be bitter
But I won't play that game.

I wash her hands and face
And comb her thinning hair
The way she always wore it
To show her that I care.

Was it losing all her eye sight
That caused her brow to frown?
Or was it pain now in her body
Or her sons down in the ground?

Was it work that made her hands wrinkled?
And was it loss that made her hard?
For Gramma never hugged us,
She kept all her feelings barred.

Was it tucking in the doctor's children
Underneath the quilt
When she gave into loving Martha
That caused her so much guilt?

Was it sadness for her siblings,
Those ten that lie in graves
From battlefields and disease
And mining like a slave?

Was it losing her second husband?
Or Mary going home?
Or Angus getting married?
Or living all alone?

As I visit her in the Institute
I think about my own life
To nearly twenty years before
When Angus took a wife.

I had been his choice
That dark-haired Mabou girl

Donelda MacDonnell

For better or for worse
We were ready to face the world.

Angus with his Irish blarney
And me with my Scottish wit
After years of all that green blood
I diluted it a bit!

Molly's days were happier now
As she watched the babies come
They re-filled her life with laughter
And she began to soften some.

She told them of her life,
Of her wants, her needs and fears
And recounted many stories
Of Walter the Pioneer.

Many months Gramma stayed
Beneath our roof with us.
I had to be on my toes
There shouldn't be any dust!

Soon Molly's care grew greater
I just didn't have the back
To care for an elderly person
I guiltily helped her pack.

Now on one of my many visits
I try to see what Molly saw
I've spent a long time caring
'Cause she is my Mother-in-law.

Obeying her simple wishes
(I had to be discreet)
She savours every crystal
Of a smuggled, forbidden treat.

She talks of going home
Is it Glencoe or is it Heaven?
'Cause the lady in the chair
Has now reached ninety-seven.

Returning now to child-like days
She eats with hands and bib
Night comes early—in a bed
With rails—just like a crib.

Tired now, she wants to sleep
So I help her to her bed
Tears trickle beside each eye
Of her tired and weary head.

But now she's tied into her crib
And resents her imperfection

She calls the nurses unkind names
And she prays for His protection.

Tucked into her flannel sheet
She lies helpless—at my inspection
And as I leave I wipe away,
Tears of true affection.

Standing by her door side
I stand for one more look
At the lady worn and wrinkled
And the toll that her life took.

I walk back in and place a kiss
On the head of silver hair
That hold all those memories,
So carefully stored in there.

How soon—we do not know
Will she lie beneath the sod?
And greet her family—young and old
When she sleeps and wakes with God.

Not for me—do I record
But for future generations
So take this poem and a cup of tea
For further concentration.

So all these facts I choose to tell
And give to you to share
So that Molly's life is not in vain
In her head of silver hair.

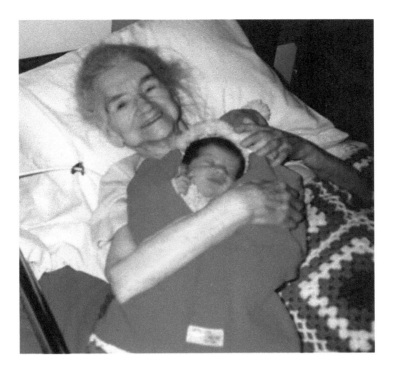

Gramma Molly, age 97 years, with infant Colin Moran

Miss Mary Ellen Moran, Mrs Hughie MacFarlane, Mrs Molly MacLean
was born Feb 28, 1893 and died on Feb 22, 1991.

Rest in Peace Gramma. You were loved.

the imprint of one

The end came fast. The timer was out of sand. All went as planned. Mama died at home surrounded by family. She was waked in the parlor. Family from 'away' flew home—the day had come for those who feared the final farewell. Children cried from lack of sleep and too much food. The wake house was filled with stories of a life short lived, a woman loved, a soul gone back to God. Beautiful Mama looked as though she were sleeping peacefully.

The long funeral procession to the church lasted for miles.

Readings in the church acclaimed a woman who loved her family and her dedication as their mother. The burial was tearful as grown sons' gloved hands placed soil on their mother's casket. A dreadful sense of loss brought brave men to tears.

Back at the house, the daughter Abby gathered the many grandchildren on the floor, next to the old dog. They began to sing a few of Gramma's favourite Gaelic songs, her own woven blankets spread across their legs. When the performance subsided, there was a heavy awkward silence. Gramma's presence remained.

Friends and strangers alike gathered to eat the scores of food provided by neighbouring hands. There was a 'wee dram' to warm their spirits. Someone played a slow lament on the fiddle. As the music quickened, sweetened hot toddies provoked the mood to match the lively tune. Lethargically smiling, the family nodded as they talked to friends, respectful to guests but now wanting to be alone.

Small clusters of friends gathered in corners and on the stairs, hugging each other. They laughed and cried about stories of this wonderful woman. Her final resolve was to make her peace with her family and with her God before she was no longer coherent. Sadly, people lingered, nervously wanting to be of some help and not knowing in what way, but offering it anyway. Women worked in the kitchen. Men stood around the doors and made small talk, only semi-skilled at the art of handling their grief in public. The wreath, indicating the wake house, still hung on the outside door. Such was, and still is, the typical sendoff for a person in Cape Breton.

Outside the moon was full and spacious; it seemed close enough that one could reach up and touch it. It lit up the yard as though it were an immense light bulb, its luminance accentuating the cars and the people who stood there. Along the hilly horizon, the slender birch trees were bare, except where little coverlets of snow lay like sleeves on their thin branches. They stood against the skyline like sentinels on guard. These bodyguards seemed too fragile to be of any usefulness, but there, in the background, they were actually quite regal.

Some family members could no longer face the throngs of people still milling about the house. This cancerous ordeal had taken nearly a year and now it was time for it to be over. Unable to allow this sadness to govern them any longer, they too lingered at the door. The silent desire in their hearts was for everyone to leave them alone now. They needed their privacy to release the sadness. They just wanted to go somewhere and scream. While they deeply appreciated people's support, the inevitable lay ahead, their lives had to go on.

Out of the blue, young Danny with a glint in his eye winked at his siblings as he nodded toward the door. He grabbed the toboggan leaning against the porch steps and with a mischievous grin, he said:

"Race you to the hill!"

Pulling his gloves from his coat pockets where they remained since he laid the first sod on his mother's wooden casket, he waved to them to follow. His siblings were astonished at such an unthinkable action, but ran behind him anyway in disbelief calling out:

"What? Danny, you can't be serious."

"C'mon", he called out, *"Mama would love it".*

Gathering their long coats up into their arms and pulling their gloves on tightly, the siblings followed him in their finery; their faces still tear-streaked from the funeral. Maury took his red tartan scarf and tied it around his waist to hold his top coat closed. They all ran behind their brother who led the way. Chasing him, they clamored:

"Come back, Danny—you must be crazy".

The girls still had on their lovely winter coats, with matching hats fitted so neatly on their heads. Bessy was in her rust-coloured woolen dress coat and Maury wore his tailored top coat, wrapped by a tartan scarf. Abby sported a matching navy coat with a light blue scarf. Danny's stylish garment was dark green with a black zipper, making his white scarf stand out. They were a handsome and impressive sight, although not appropriately dressed for tobogganing.

Grabbing the rope of another sled they chased up the hill behind him. Placing their boots in the fresh snow, they kicked out a path for each other to follow in. The indent of one became the foothold for the others.

Positioning themselves, they urged the cold wooden sleighs forward. The cool snow sprayed onto their faces, awakening their spirits, and their blood began to race. They, like the scrawny trees that had seemed so fragile, surely had vigor now.

They ascended and descended the hill, their angry energy perishing in the cold. The two pairs of brothers and sisters pulled their sleighs up the hilly mounds until they reached the crown where they had played as children. They tobogganed for a long time on that snowy hill, coasting freely to the bottom of the slope, falling over and then getting up to do the same, again and again.

They remembered when Mama was waiting with dinner cooked for them at home. Mama, with her apron on and her hair not yet combed, because she was too busy. Mama. How they loved her. Mama.

They shivered from the cold but were hot and motivated by the adrenalin that pulsed through their veins. Wiping wet noses on their sleeves, they climbed and slid, climbed and slid, their hot tears freezing on their eyelashes. They placed the steel runners in the tracks they had broken and flew to the bottom of the hill. They rolled over onto their sides, laughing and crying at the same time. Each time the wooden sleds swept snow in their faces, they resolved to go back again, just one more time, for Mama. Together the foursome fell onto their sides on a bed of crumpled snow at the bottom of the hill. Finally they lay still. Wrapped in each other's arms, they pressed against each other and cried out their grief. Through their blurred vision, they watched the kaleidoscope of stars twinkling in the still winter sky. Emotionally spent, they would now accept the truth. Mama was gone.

The clean snow washed away the memory of the days filled with sadness. They were exhausted from the work of pulling the sleighs up the hill, but exhilarated by the fast trips down. They had begun to wear off the anticipatory grief that hung over them for over a year. Together, they made their solid resolution to tolerate life now, without their beloved mother.

Eventually, one by one, headlights in the yard could be seen leaving the wake house. Smiling in the cloudy sky, the moon appeared to enjoy their play. Slowly, the young adults started their walk home, pulling their toboggans behind them, lighter now; their fine clothes were crumpled and caked with balls of snow. Too tired to talk, red faced and sweating from their work, they again placed their boots onto the path they had just made, the path that would lead them home again. Disheveled and ruddy, they entered into the warmth of the kitchen, welcomed gladly by their family and a few close friends. They laughed as they told of their impromptu sledding. Everyone remarked how Mama would have laughed, how she would have said:

*"Well, that's life, get on with it, and move your arse. You can't stop living, just put one foot in front of the other and get on with your **life**."*

She would have emphasized the word 'life'.

They had managed the day, using her own spirit and determination as the only way they knew how to keep going. Heartily laughing, these young adults settled into the late evening with hot tea and cold faces, warmed by the heat of the fire. Fat slices of homemade brown raisin bread smothered with her own preserves were served up, her presence still so real that it was easy to forget she was gone. Their heartbroken father enjoyed the story of the late night tobogganing trip.

Their grief did not evaporate overnight. Often, after a long day's work, one boy would not return to the house in time for supper, but only later, with nasal stuffiness and eyes full of sorrow. The sounds of his gulping cries could be heard. That same moon silhouetted the shape of a young man, holding his head in his hands. More often, as was their way, the girls were more visible with their pain, openly wiping away tears, as this was more acceptable in the clan. More acceptable as well, was the habit of the grown brothers to again take the lead and protect their sisters with great armfuls of affection. It was a perfect balance.

The memory of the impromptu tobogganing session was salted away in the stories that Mama drew from so many times. Now it was considered among the best. But it was never to be told among some people. They would not be able to understand it was a deep love and not disrespect that caused them to revert to their childhood passion. To search for a mother's presence, even in her absence, to an earlier time when Mama was there to receive them after they had finished their play.

Now they could face the world. They were unaware of the stages of grief and the psychology of mourning and loss. They would carry on, because of people who had passed along the wisdom to do so.

The moonlight had smiled on the actions of the young people. Those feeble looking trees had saluted on guard. Across their thin shadows, the young people had moved freely down the snowcapped hills. They created a new path to follow and had left their mark for others to find their own firm footing. These siblings filtered and cleansed their pain by the cold air and snow. They had followed the imprint of good role models and left footholds for others.

Do you have a footprint of behavior you admire and follow? Life can be an uphill battle. Sometimes you just have to grab that sleigh and get away. The ride home might be exhilarating! Perhaps you can recall a time when you had to pick up your sleigh and head for the hills?

The Dance

Convoys of vehicles converge at the little hall in the centre of the woods. Music flows, ripples and crashes much like the water that trickles and cascades over rocks in a river. Carrying joy through the air in every direction, the strings call the faithful to 'The Dance'. For generations, summer and winter, people happily exit their vehicles and enter the open door. Inside the little hall, the wooden floor visibly bounces as hundreds of feet pound in rhythm with the fiddle music, while sweat discolors every shirt. Sleeves are rolled up and pant legs quiver as the men 'drive'er' to the music. With equal stamina, women step the intricate formations too. The piano player's fingers blur as they race up and down, back and forth, over the ebony and ivory keys.

Glencoe Mills Church & Hall: Margie MacDonald Photography

People move in rhythm to the familiar choreographed movements of The Dance, gleefully screaming guttural sounds as would prisoners released into the free world. The unstoppable screams expel, literally spring right up from the bottom of the lungs. It is the very best cardiac workout exercise and the most fun a person could ever have. This exact colourful scenario happens often in every hall on the little island of Cape Breton, but especially in Glencoe Mills. There are few things more loved than the Cape Breton Square Dance. Emotions stir to complete euphoria at the sound of the bow passing over taut violin strings, luring people onto the floor. Many the story has been told by people driving from Toronto and arriving just in time for The Dance in Glencoe Mills! Just to hear master-fiddler Buddy MacMaster, who played for over thirty years and felt he didn't own the music, we did.

Moving in and out, twisting and turning in all directions, the dancers flow in and out with the same rhythm as a river, sparking with clean and noisy joy. People have to be loose when they dance, not stiffly holding their bodies. Heads bob, arms swing, ankles are rubber. Even older, heavy men hardly touch the floor when they dance if they are 'light on their feet'. My great-grandfather 'Big Dan' Cameron was known as the best dancer in his time, so lightly did he step. There are three figures in a set. The first two figures are gentle dancing to a jig, with people flowing in and out and swaying about.

During the third figure, the fiddler would suddenly put the 'dirt' into the reel. Adjusting posture and grasping the violin, the fiddler holds the instrument tighter under the chin and digs in. When a fiddler cranked it up a notch, the real steps began!

The master of the fiddle sits on a hard four-legged wooden chair; sweat ripples down his face as he coaxes, then forces astonishing sounds with the narrow bow that dances and saws on tight fiddle strings. His legs bounce high as he thumps both feet in time with the music. The piano player sits with his or her back to the people. Men hold their ladies' hand up in the air as she twirls beneath, in these highly organized formations. Newcomers, unfamiliar with this tradition, wonder how this is all possible, with one and

Charcoal drawing of Mary Janet's dancing shoes and Rodney MacDonald's fiddle

all moving about in every direction, but in perfect unison. If they decide to dance, they are expected to follow all the same moves.

Few things in Cape Breton are as important as The Dance. Regional dancing includes vestiges of French and English quadrilles and lancers. The Cape Breton reels have evolved to include step dancing that came from Scotland with our ancestors and still lives on today.

The population of approximately 95,000 people in Cape Breton swells by thousands in the summer months. Freshly cooked lobsters and Celtic music signal all Cape Bretoners to come Home. The generosity of people and their friendliness, combined with the beauty of the Island seizes the hearts of visitors. The natural beauty, the pace and the space are what brings tourists here; it's the people who bring them back. And the Dance.

Cape Breton Island is joined to the mainland of Nova Scotia by the Canso Causeway, which was completed in 1955. Cape Breton Island is divided into four counties: Cape Breton, Inverness, Richmond, and Victoria. Derivatives of the name Glengarry are widely used; every community has a Glen, one even has a distillery that makes Glen Breton whiskey. All areas display such breath-taking beauty, people are often heard to say in awe:

IT JUST DOESN'T GET ANY BETTER THAN THIS

Over an area of nearly 4,000 square miles, the Island has several main cultures: Dutch, Mi'kmaq, French and Scots (or Gaels) and the Irish. No matter the diversity, they all love to square dance! However, unless 'it's in your blood' the steps don't come as easily but still are so much fun. Everyone is smiling, laughing and hollering because the pure joy instilled by the music brings about agility that has to be felt to be believed. If you can hear Natalie MacMaster play *The King's Reel* without tapping your foot, you need to take your pulse.

Some of the Scottish people who crossed the Atlantic some two hundred years ago seeking a better life came from the Lochaber region (such are the ancestors of this writer). Documents show the long trip was cruel and surreal with horrific conditions and many deaths. The ships were known as coffin ships as people sailed to their deaths in poorly constructed boats.

Children born to Scottish settlers and their descendants are known as Gaels, some of whom still speak Gaelic. The language is still taught in schools here.

Hardy and determined, Celtic people are generally not openly amorous. A little kiss on their wedding day would be all the sexual expression the public would ever see. After a dozen or so children, it was assumed they were more expressive in private! Characteristics of clans are recognized and people will say, *"Well, it's in your people to have that skill"*. Most people know and love their own clan tartan. Gaelic singing is often heard. I'm one who won't turn the car radio off when there's a good tune playing. It's just wonderful to be of Celtic descent!

A LITTLE BIT OF HISTORY

Some of this information is taken from *The Broken Ground* by the late Ned MacDonald of Inverness, Cape Breton, a great writer[2]. These Highland farming families in Scotland had been renting land they could never own. Their houses were built stone by stone, by hand, on soil that was mostly rock and bog. They struggled to work the land for generations before they were suddenly expropriated. Their homes were taken over for cattle and sheep. It was known as the 'Clearances.' This expulsion would be considered ethnic cleansing today. They could not be suppressed though; broken-hearted, they left by boat to cross the Atlantic. A number of Scottish families, mostly Roman Catholic, arrived in Nova Scotia in the late 1700s from the Western Isles (the Hebrides). Many took up land near Antigonish, others along the Bay of Fundy near Parrsboro, and some later moved to Cape Breton Island. Around the year 1800, a number of other families emigrated from Barra in the Hebrides, settling along the Bras d'Or Lakes where they established communities with strong connections based on a mutual kinship and their shared language.

Boatloads arrived on the Eastern coast of Canada. Many stayed right where they landed and many more moved upward to Ontario and into the United States. They were able to receive land grants, which would become

[2]Ned MacDonald, *The Broken Ground: A history of Inverness Town 1803–1954.* Privately published, 1979, 60pp. Illus. Map. History with emphasis on coal mining.

their homesteads. No doubt the first to arrive had the worst of times and they in turn housed those who would follow later. Their letters to their relatives 'back home' in Scotland told of the beautiful, bounteous land in Cape Breton. These resourceful pioneers cleared the trees, tilled the land and dug for water by hand. They built their homes and barns and fought hard to stabilize their lives, as successful immigrants always do. Once settled, they would immediately build a church. And, of course, a 'still' was a must!

They became Canadian citizens. They 'set up housekeeping' as married couples and raised large families, all brought up as faith-filled Christians. The name Nova Scotia is Latin for 'New Scotland,' and was first given to this part of North America in 1621. It's such a rich and interesting history.

Although there were occasional Scots among the early settlers, they did not come in large numbers or establish permanent communities until the late 1700s, when emigrants from the north-western coast of Scotland arrived in Pictou. The Pictou Scots were Presbyterian and spoke Scottish Gaelic. Pictou continues to celebrate the arrival of the ship *Hector* with its founding immigrants.

In 1775 Captain Michael MacDonald came to the western shore of Cape Breton Island and encouraged his family and friends to join him in the area now known as Inverness County. They welcomed the opportunity to acquire their own land and begin farming and fishing. Thus began Scottish settlement on Cape Breton Island.

Each summer, and especially during the *Celtic Colours International Festival* in October, there are countless opportunities to enjoy traditional dancing, singing, piping and story-telling, as well as to meet local people and hear Gaelic spoken and sung. Gaels in Nova Scotia have always treasured the hospitality of their ancestors, and today they extend *Cead Mile Failte* (One Hundred Thousand Welcomes) to all visitors, particularly those who may be distant kin. But most important is The Dance.

The land in Cape Breton was such rich soil, these new settlers could scarcely believe their good fortune. They were quick to sow the seeds and plants brought with them, that would grow into enough harvest to last long winters. People shared and helped out with barn and house building and bartered meat for wheat in some cases. Log mills were built; coopers (barrel makers) and carpenters plied their trades. They prepared planks from logs and cut and hauled trees. Seeds for vegetables and flowers were grown and shared. Women took their recipes, the men took their tools, and all took their skills. They took their strong faith; Catholics settling mostly in Cape Breton and Protestants on the mainland of Nova Scotia.

AND...THEY BROUGHT THEIR MUSIC

They knew the music so well, they could jig a tune, mouthing songs in their deep Gaelic brogue. (Thuh, Thum, Diddle, dum, deedle deedle deedle diddle!) Some Irish people could play the tin-whistle or flute and others could play the fiddle. Bagpipes were always a welcome addition, putting voice to both mournful and cheerful times. The powerful and sorrowful sounds are best appreciated *outside*! Hearing the bagpipes always brings about a feeling of strong pride and deep respect in me. The sound makes me inhale deeply, stand taller and appreciate the connection to our ancestors.

Weekends always had a dance but never on Sunday as that was the Lord's Day. Weddings often included dances outdoors, on large boards. The last day of haymaking or barn building was the perfect time to celebrate with a square dance. Prompters would call the motions of the sets, which they literally sang the words to in tune with the music.

Natalie MacMaster. Photo: Sean Purser
Dawn and Margie Beaton. Photo: Neil Gascoyne
Used by permission of Celtic Colours
International Festival

No matter how weary, the action of rubbing and pounding the soles of the feet on the earth rejuvenated even the most fatigued. Lifelong friendships were made, courting began and marriages developed from 'The Dance'. Fiddlers often had to change their sweaty clothes several times during each dance; such was the work of playing for hours on end. A little drink helped draw the best tunes out of the players, who were mostly men, but not entirely.

So many people left Scotland that step dancing was forgotten and incredibly had to be restored by Cape Bretoners of Scottish descendants. For many years Mary Janet MacDonald, step dancer, and renowned fiddler Buddy

MacMaster would travel to Scotland bringing the steps of their ancestors back to them.

The early settlers brought their Gaelic language, which is still spoken and taught in schools. Even those with very little knowledge of the Gaelic language can respond to the question "*Ciamar a tha thu*?" (How are you?) and know that "*Cead míle fáilte*" is a hundred thousand welcomes.

THE WAY 'THE DANCE' GOES

The Dance is comprised of three separate parts, called figures, which is called 'dancing a square set'.

The first figure is danced to a jig—people dance either forward and back or do the 'shuffle' and then dance with their corner partner—that's all that's done in the first figure—this happens about four times in the first figure and usually when they've danced the four parts of the first figure—people in the set clap their hands in time to the music to indicate to the fiddler (who a lot of the time isn't watching—but playing with their eyes closed) that they've danced the four parts and it's time to stop.

Second Figure—also danced to a jig—people dance either forward and back in a circle or do the shuffle again—and then dance with their partner—and promenade to the right. Then repeat but next time promenade to the left—and then repeat all that once again so that the pattern happens four times; then the second figure ends the same way as the first—with the dancers clapping in time to the music to tell the fiddler it's time to stop.

Third Figure—danced to a reel—starts with right hand to your partner and then left to next etc. and you do a 'half grand chain' until you meet your partner. Then, swing your partner, go back, until you meet your partner. Then, promenade—'faces the music' when they get to the stage, they turn towards one another and head back through all the couples that are lined up. When they get to the back of the hall, they 'cast-off'—gents one way—ladies the other—until they all are lined up. Dancers go forward and back in this long string and some come 'back on er' step dancing. They all step dance toward their partners and get their set back into a 'circle', and that's the first quarter of the set. Each step has a name such as 'back step' or 'shuffle'.

They then repeat the very same moves as above, only the next time the head couple, or any couple, 'face the back of the hall'. That takes you to the first 'half' of the set. Then—the first quarter and the second quarter of the set (just described) is repeated once again. This makes up four parts of the third figure. To end the figure, instead of 'half grand chain' the couples do a 'full grand chain' or go 'all the way'. This means they pass their partner by. When they get to their partner—they don't swing this time—instead they promenade around and all join hands in the circle. Now everybody step dances or goes forward and back (if they can't step dance) and this ends the third figure. Now the dancers disperse—and it's the only figure where the dancers don't clap to end the set—they just disperse—wiping their brow—and the men get ready to seek out their next partner.

It takes very little to follow, once a person has danced one set. It's such a wonderful thing to do people literally cannot control the screams of delight that burst forth. If it sounds complicated in print, it's not a bit in reality. People kindly lead a newcomer through one set, which immediately leaves them anxious to do it all again. Step dancing is a gift given to us by our Scottish ancestors and is respected throughout Cape Breton as such.

From time to time when the floor would be cleared, a particularly good dancer would solo perform, much to the delight of the crowd, showing appreciation with their claps and screams! The fiddler will start a strathspey, which is a 'call' to solo dancers in the hall to come out. They give a step or two—and only a short demo from each one. There is an unwritten rule that they will give a chance to other dancers in the crowd, and to not to wear out the fiddler. Once the strathspey turns into a reel, sometimes up to 15 dancers will come out. And sometimes, as well, just to give everyone a break—maybe once in the evening, and after a particularly sweaty square set—the fiddler will launch into a beautiful waltz and couples 'round-dance' around the hall.

In days gone by, the dancer, like the fiddler would have their best dress-clothes on; for the men it was a suit and tie. They wore hard-soled leather, laced shoes, which gave a sharp sound to the steps. Things have changed a lot and clothing is much more casual now. Women wore skirts and blouses then, even colorful pleated skirts when during the dance, the pleats would fan open and then fold again. What a beautiful sight to see!

Some steps were particularly eloquent, one foot quickly darting over the other, in front of the other foot, and then behind in great speed. Even men who had worked in greasy trucks, barns or fields all day would shower, shave and wear dress pants and their good leather shoes. This was in respect for the public affair and to make the best steps. It was to impress the ladies too. The behaviours of the dance were well understood.

Few things in Cape Breton are as popular as the dance of the Gaels. Grandparents take their little grandchildren to learn the figures, and maneuver the many changes in the sets. Brothers take their sisters, kids jiggle around everywhere. The same traditions have continued without change for generations. The music gets into the veins, leaving no choice but to dance. Hoping someone will ask for a dance, women's eyes search for their favourite partner. A few late starters stand at the door, having that last puff of a cigarette. Or more realistically, a swig of rum, always guaranteed to bring the best steps, until too much destroys the whole set. Older ladies line the walls in the chairs placed there just for them. Perhaps too crippled to dance anymore or in fear of falling, they watch, in awe of all the sights and sounds before them. They closely observe who danced with whom and what everyone wore as it would be fodder for the following week's gossip! If a man asked the same gal for two sets, they were as good as married! When a man asked to take a lady home, he surely had the 'noisean' for her. That information was not lost on the crowd!

No one refused a set with a veteran. Revered in every community, even young people shook hands to show respect for their sacrifice. Great efforts were made to show respect to those who didn't come home. The returnees were and are special guests at any event. The history of the wars has always been of great interest to the local people.

So it was of great curiosity in the late '60s and early '70s when a group of people came to Cape Breton. They were draft dodgers who left the United States to escape going to war. Though it was strange to the staunch Cape Breton people to understand folks refusing to fight for their country, they accepted these strangers and helped them to adjust to rural living. These people were ordinary folks, not criminals, and brave for wanting to live in the back woods, in a way our forefathers fought to overcome.

In Cape Breton, it was hard to understand people who dodged the draft. Loyalty to their country was a huge matter to Canadians, who didn't have a choice; they were conscripted. Many U.S. draft dodgers came to Cape Breton during the Vietnam War era. The 'Burn Your Bra' revolution had already started in the U.S., where the young and educated protested against any structured society. They considered religion and government as control tactics and they rallied hard against it.

So, they fled to Canada, a place where they would be protected, to have a 'back to the land' experience. But also where their lifestyle would be so different from the local people who worked hard to rise up from poverty. These 'dodgers' communed together and lived without most amenities of life. They were proud of their draft papers and showed them to anyone who cared to see them. Wanting to shake off the restraints of society, some preferred to be naked while on their own property and never shy when visitors came by. The skunky smell of weed hung in the air. Their lives were a study in contrast to the structure of the Gaels and the Irish who had fled their countries to find a place to live.

Perhaps a bit envious that these folks could choose an alternate lifestyle, the generous Cape Breton people respected their decisions and adopted a helpful attitude, knowing they would be in for a hard time, being unprepared for the harsh winters. Angus (Dunmore) Beaton took his divining rod and found water for them. Others helped them clear an area for a road. People showed them how to plant a garden. Each group considered the other to be unique. Simple reasoning perhaps, but each decided to just accept each other. Several couples lived together in an old house in the woods with their philosophies, their changing partners and a growing brood of kids. Cleverly, they obtained tools and amazed people with their workmanship skills. They were eventually employed by the local people, who came to admire their skills, if not their lifestyles. Religious beliefs were not important, and neither was marriage or personal hygiene. Even the heavy aroma of garlic could not hide the odour of uncleanliness.

They drew stares at the little Co-op in Port Hood and took all this in stride. Their oversized red and black-checkered jackets in summer seemed out of place, as did their lack of clothing at other events. They were not mean, vulgar, or violent. They just simply wanted to live off the land as best they could. People respected that and liked them as individuals.

One very gentle lady was a potter and created the most beautiful dishes. Many of her pieces still remain; indeed I have several. They made ceramic counter tops and built kitchen cupboards. Uniquely intriguing, they were still widely accepted by the people.

For years, they grew to know the struggles of winter, cutting wood for their stoves, hauling water for cooking and washing children's clothes. They were not nasty, rather they were gentle folk who simply wanted a pioneer lifestyle. They would wait out the war and see what happened. Local people, true to their kind nature, helped them in every way. They simply became known as 'The Hippies'. Other dissenters across Canada were accepted in like manner and were always grateful to those who helped them. They were welcomed in every way.

UNTIL...THEY SHOWED UP AT THE DANCE

Heads turned! The ole lady crowd leaned toward each other muttering, *"...well, will you look at the head on that!"* Hair was the most astonishing aspect of them. Piled high on their heads, the men had big bushy ponytails and large overgrown beards. They wore denim coveralls ripped to the knee, naked underneath. Some just wore Stanfield's long underwear, open to the groin. Neck bindings often lost elasticity so one side hung across their shoulder, revealing a nipple. People stared and gawked in amazement. The stark contrast was not missed by the 'ole lady gang'.

They wore gumboots or rubber boots with long woolen socks. They drew the curiosity, if not the ire of the local dancers. They didn't wear underwear, another protest against the restraints of organized society. The girls had long, loosely braided hair with sun-dried wisps sticking in every direction. Often one gal held a baby on her hip, nursing while she danced! Whoever was holding the baby also nursed it! The women wore little summer dresses, so thin they were almost translucent. Some wore large straw hats frayed all around the edges. Their amorous displays of affection shocked the modest Celtic people.

Compared to tightly maneuvered steps danced in laced leather shoes, they wore rubber boots, stood on one foot and kicked the other in front or behind them. Or, they took itty bitty teeny tiny steps, going nowhere! People stared whispering in astonishment *"...what in the hell are they doing?"* They kicked their booted legs high in the air. They did a sort of clogging or jumping on the spot while others wandered about randomly, completely out of tune with the speed of the music. Doing something akin to the chicken walk, they bobbed their heads, while others seemed to be pole dancing, without the pole! Hands on their hips, they bounced, jumped, leaped and jerked around. One fellow even played his harmonica! They were a sight, neither rowdy nor rambunctious, just giving the peace sign as they moved about in a trance.

Young men watched carefully as a youthful breast often poked out from under the coveralls. Or when legs were kicked high exposing bare bums. No effort was made to hide body parts and this 'rubber boot brigade' made sure their shocking behaviour was seen by all.

The neatly trimmed and clean-shaven men of CB contrasted starkly to hairy man buns and full grown, unkempt beards. Their neat steps juxtaposed the haphazard movements of these newcomers. The long facial hairs sprouted sprigs of straw and hayseed in their dreadlocks. This was a marked difference to the neatly preened hair of the Cape Breton men. These people from the commune were flower children, with children, and were going to party wherever and however they wanted. High on home-grown weed, their actions were seen as bizarre at The Dance: running on the spot, reaching into the air, kicking one foot at a time high in front of them. Their disorganized behavior moved into the sets and were not appreciated. Neither were their hairy armpits! They ruined every single dance they attended.

Let this be a cautionary tale—don't mess with our dance, we will never forget! They lived here for years, and were very clever in getting government grants to set up businesses. They are mostly gone now. But they will never be forgotten.

Meanwhile, the dancing remains and is as structured as ever; however, female fiddlers are more common now. Male fiddlers can be seen with their caps on backwards, wearing both a kilt and work-boots and often accompanied by a guitar player. Keyboards are used now. Step dancers have modernized a lot too, wearing sneakers or even dancing barefoot. One can see people wearing shorts and even less in a set. And it's not unusual to see women dancing with each other now. Nor is it uncommon to see fiddlers step dance while playing the fiddle and that's an incredible sight. Several musicians even turn around in circles as they play the fiddle and literally skip left across the stage in one direction, then right on the other. People still scream in delight! It's pure amazement to see 'Kenny's boys' from Mabou Harbour all line up and step dance together.

Ceilidhs are more portable now, with keyboards and so many young musicians. Dancers have even more agility than they originally showed, often leaning forward, and bringing the knees high.

We never learn. War is never the way to peace. The draft dodgers may have been right in their philosophy, but they sure couldn't square dance! Neither did they try; the little Glencoe Mills hall was just a place to go to party.

Their legacy was limited but ours has persevered; the music and culture is strong. What hasn't changed is the picturesque landscape of green lush hills, meadows and clean communities and beaches. Our musical connection to Scotland is our pride. The convoys of dusty vehicles still travel the roads to the little halls in the woods, the old lady watch patrol and the respect we have for our veterans is still here. And our gratitude to the brave people who crossed the treacherous ocean to become our Canadian ancestors and bring us The Dance!

The Rawleigh Man

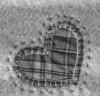

During the Canadian war years, while my mother waited for her soldier-love to return from Europe, she worked in Halifax, Nova Scotia. Among other jobs, she worked in the Moirs chocolate factory, where she grew to dislike the very smell and taste of chocolate. She told me many stories of how, through their sorrow, they still had fun as she and her girlfriends worked and waited for their boyfriends to return from overseas. When he returned, Annie Margaret and Donald were married.

The expectation was that women would stop working and return to the home to be wives and mothers. So after the war ended, she and my father married and started a family, where naturally she would go into the home and start having babies.

And so it was that she began her life in the private sphere as wife and mother to her eight children. The little home she made in Mabou must have been a stark contrast to her life in Halifax, but similar to the life she knew as a child in the beautiful Coal Mines. She joyfully began her life where hard work and creative improvisation had to be a way of life for many mothers. I remember that my mother slaved in our home. Her work began early every day, standing over a wringer washer or a hot wood stove, making many loaves of bread and pots of stew and pickles, not to mention the Christmas fruit-

cakes! I remember with respect, those women on our street who always wore house-dresses, silk slips and nylons, even on the hottest of days, whether they were pregnant or not. My mother never knew the freedom of wearing slacks.

The work that these women did was unpaid and unvalued to the world but essential to the successful operation of the home. Their day did not end with nightfall as there were responsibilities to visitors and children who could not begin to understand the contributions women made. Any social-ization for these women was done with each other, comparing the lives that mirrored each other. There were no luxuries, not even stores for them to shop in, except for Beaton's Clothing where Mary was sure to '...charge the taxes...!' But I still can remember how a little bit of the 'store' would come to us.

I was the fourth child to come into the family of eight children. I recall that it was a really big deal when the distributor for Rawleigh products would come to the village. When the 50 or more children on Back Street knew the Rawleigh Man was at one house, we would run as fast as our legs would carry us, just to be the first to tell the big news to our mothers. We didn't know why it was big news, we just knew it was really important to them.

The Rawleigh Man was a short, round man who carried a leather brief-case and had a very calming presence about him. He seemed to arrive at regular intervals to visit the mothers and supply the items they could not get at the local grocers. When he came to our house, my mother would clear

away the sugar-dish, the butter-dish, and the salt and pepper shakers from the centre of the kitchen table. When he opened up the suitcase, a mixture of aromas escaped into the air. He would lay the items out on the table, one by one. The plastic tablecloth had the flowers nearly worn off, from my mother kneading bread and rolling out pie crusts day after day. While she cleared the space for him, she would anxiously ask him if he had 'such and such' product, relaying to him the information about who benefited from what item—for what ailment.

One product he was sure to have consisted of small round cans of medicated ointment. One tin container was silver with royal blue printing on it. It was camphorated salve. My mother would rub it on our backs and heat it up for us to inhale when we were sick.

When it was all gone, it was certain to be replaced by another, and the empty can would be saved to store small miscellaneous items like buttons, pins and perhaps a snip of a baby's first haircut.

Another product was in a similar can, except that it was a gold-coloured can with black lettering on it and had brown medicated salve in it. It was used for the many mosquito bites and smaller wounds that were constantly coming in the door for my mother to fix. I put it on every cat in town. It was the magic elixir, real or imagined; every home had to have this ointment.

The Rawleigh Man also sold pie fillings. My mother always got the boxes of lemon and butterscotch flavors. That night we usually had the homemade pie for dessert, with thick meringue on top, browned in a hot oven, for a very few moments only! Along with the pie fillings, he offered concentrated drinks in a tall glass bottle. One capful would make a delicious cool drink, somewhat like a glass of pop would taste today. Lime was the regular purchase. Real vanilla, (not to be confused with vanilla extract), and lemon extract were other products my mother would definitely get for her baking. Except for some face cream from the Avon Lady, I do not recall her buying personal items, just cooking supplies.

I do not remember if it was the Rawleigh Man who carried these items, but my mother used to get me a horrific tasting liquid called Scott's Emulsion to stimulate my appetite. I was very skinny then and she tended to worry about that. Thankfully, the emulsion was replaced by a thick, brown, sweeter tasting supplement. (Forty years later, I can testify that both products have kicked in very well.) I also had to take cod-liver-oil capsules for whatever reason, I still don't know, except to say my mother took her parenting very seriously.

When Mr. Rawleigh Man had finished his sale, my mother would ask him to stay for tea. First she would move the kettle onto the hottest part of the wood stove, where it soon began to steam. The shiny surface of the stove had been polished with wax paper. Going to the left side of the kitchen, she would remove the 'good' cups off the little hooks from where they hung in the pantry. Taking a clean cup, she would wipe the best cup out (in case there might be a bit of dust there) and place it on its matching saucer. Being a precision conscious person, it was important to her that the yellow flower design on the teacup was placed perfectly above the coordinating flowers on the plate. Two Red Rose tea bags went into the little silver teapot. She stirred it occasionally, keeping it very hot, but being careful not to let it boil. When it was properly brewed, the steaming tea was poured into the thin edged cup, with a little milk poured in first. A slender round sugar cookie, a biscuit, homemade cheese and a bowl of strawberry-rhubarb jam would be placed on a tea plate beside his teacup. My mother would shyly apologize for not having very much to offer him. If he had been an official Sunday visitor, he would have sat in the parlor, but he never made it that far, being a salesman.

He had to endure this ritual at each home, for fear he would offend the women. Today I know why he was so round and peaceful—he was stuffed! I often wonder how my mother would pay for these items, as she did not have a pay cheque or a bank account. Likely, the visits were synchronized with the arrival of the Baby Bonus cheques and the money was to be divvied out carefully and accounted for by her.

Among my many memories of life on Back Street, the Rawleigh Man stands out as a welcome symbol of how the world of products came into my mother's little kitchen in Mabou. As few and insignificant as they may appear to us today, they pleased her to be able to perfect her art of cooking and baking for her family and guests.

My mother has been absent from my life for too many years now and I miss her more every day. I want her here for many reasons. She would be pleased to know the Scott's Emulsion has worked and that I was watching how she sewed because I learned that skill from her. Other reasons would be to record her memories of her life as a girl in the Coal Mines, her work in Halifax, and as a young bride and then a mother on Back Street in Mabou. I tend to gravitate toward women who would be her age and ask them about their lives. It is the only way to find out what she would be like if she were here with us today.

If she were only here, she could meet my children and vice versa. She could answer all the questions that they ask me about myself when I was their ages, and tell me more about things like the opportunities and the hardships that made her life what it was. I would help perm her hair and take her for her appointments. I would tell her how I remember what she did for us and how much I appreciate it now. I would show her how much I love her. Although my mother is gone, the memory of her labour of love lives on respectfully in my heart.

A Promise Kept

Joe's long legs lumbered quickly down the hospital steps. He yanked open the door of the old truck. It had been a long day for the carpenter. Holding a smoke in one side of his mouth, he cupped it with his left hand, lit it with his right and blew the first puff as he reached for his phone.

"Helen, I won't be home for supper tonight; save a plate for me though," he told his surprised wife.

"I was just in to see Michael."

"And now I have to go to Arichat."

He had just stopped in to the Palliative Care Unit to visit his good friend Michael, who struggled with cancer the last three years. He thought it would be a short visit. Michael, asking to speak to him privately, had given a lot of thought to this meeting. Joseph imagined he would be asked to be a pallbearer. However, this final farewell would turn into a surprise last minute request. Closing the hospital room door, the good friends greeted each other; one stood tall, suntanned and strong, the other, his friend on his deathbed, was bald and thin.

"Awweh, Michael" he said, *"...it's good to see you,"* taking the small frail hand in his own. It was then that Michael revealed he didn't want his widow spending much-needed money on an expensive funeral. Would Joseph agree to make his casket? Shocked, Joseph immediately understood the concern, as Michael was leaving his wife with three young children. Pained at the reality of the situation, Joseph assured him:

"Don't you worry about a thing my friend."

"I'll take care of that for you."

Their own private conversation followed. Leaving the room, Joseph met the palliative care nurse.

"Michael just asked me to make his casket."

"You better hurry." she replied, *"He doesn't have much time."*

It was Thursday evening. Descending the hospital stairs, he wondered how he was going to do this project, or if he'd even have time. Mentally ciphering what he'd need, Joseph was careful driving as a severe ice storm had gripped the area. Profoundly shocked, the resolve to meet a dying man's wish was equal in measure. Posited with such an earnest request from a dying man with sores in and around his mouth, it was impossible to refuse.

"Yes, I'll do that for you Michael. You don't have to worry about a thing. I'll take care of that for you".

The late trip was a pensive one for the carpenter. His neighbour and friend was dying. Such sadness...such a great man, father and husband, lawyer and fiddle player. Such a shame. From time to time, as he drove in the darkness Joseph would say his name out loud...Michael.

Visualizing the finished project, he immediately knew what he'd do. Wide mahogany boards would be stained for the shell. The four corners would be dovetailed. The two-piece top would be flat. What about the hardware and how would he fashion the corners? What about the inside? What about measurements? He resolved to use every skill to keep his promise. There would be no velvet brocade casket with ugly steel handles for Michael, a man who enjoyed the simplicities of life. His final resting place would not contradict; rather, it would reflect the earthiness of the man.

So many thoughts, so tired already, he faced the old green GMC in the direction of the supply yard in Pondville, a tiny community in Cape Breton. Did he have enough money? Mentally calculating, his thoughts estimated the design as well as the cost.

Memories of taking their kids to the beach simultaneously filled his mind. Long talks on hot summer evenings over a brew, story after story, ach, what a shame the man is dying.

With a mixture of sadness and fond memories, the promise would consume his thoughts on that long, nasty icy drive. He would see the man with the saw mill who cut logs and sold boards. Hearing the favour his friend Joseph was about to grant him, the lawyer would accept no money for the goods. Mutually understanding, their manly handshake clinched the exchange.

Michael was an apt storyteller and played the fiddle. What he really loved was the choir where he practiced hymns for Mass. For as long as he could, he loyally sang with his friends, until he couldn't. The time came when he told them he could no longer sing with them; then lovingly and with much peace and joy, he calmly smiled: *"Well, not this choir anyway. I'll be singing in the Heavenly Choir".* Such was his strong Catholic faith.

Arriving late to home that night, Joseph took the long boards off the truck and placed them in his workshop. Even at that late hour, his wife had supper ready; he ate and went to bed, hardly sleeping as work would come early.

The next work day was long; he had a bite to eat when he got home. Coffee in hand, he headed to his shop where the carpentry work began... measuring, cutting, sanding and gluing. After scribbling a few measurements on a small piece of wood, the hand carving of the joints began. More sanding, measuring, nailing, then pulling the grain out from the wood with stain. Making the image he had seen in his mind, a thing of beauty began to take shape among the shavings curled on the floor. The sweet smell of cut wood mixed with odors of stain and varnish that wafted through the dusty air. It was now Friday.

The handmade dovetailed corners were glued and fitted inside each other. The light and dark stained grains in the wood complemented one another. After another full day of cutting, clamping and varnishing, the stained wood looked pretty darn good to the carpenter! Stunning, really! With his pencil tucked behind one ear, cap tipped on the back of his head, smoke curling upward from his ever present smokes, the builder would make the most beautiful casket he could. He was honouring his own word as well as his friend's last request.

Questions remained: What could he do for the inside? Who can help? He called the only one he thought could adequately upholster and line the interior of a casket. She lived nearby and was a good friend. She sewed for herself and others and was game for most projects. Similarly, as soon as she heard the story, she sensed his urgency so her response was like his own and she immediately said, *"Sure Joseph, I'll do that".*

In an equally similar conundrum, she wondered, *"Hmm, everything's closed, no supplies, what could be used?"* Deep down, she thought, *"How in the Name of God do I line a casket?"*

Both the carpenter and the seamstress had the same thought: if you're going to do it, do it right! Their people had been tough, hardworking, and capable. Most important to them, a promise was a promise and your word as good as a legal document. They were determined it would get done.

The lady from the quilt shop supplied the fabric for a curtain that would hang from the top of the inside of the box, which would be padded first with soft quilt batting and stapled to the inside. The gorgeous cotton fabric, cream coloured with tiny complementary matching flowers, would be gathered three to four times the length to make the fullness of the curtain. This interior panel would surround the entire circumference of the inside of the casket. She undertook this project, mentally rotating the pattern in her head, before the first cut was even made.

Both worked together, apart; he in his workshop and she in her home, creating quickly to meet the looming deadline.

Now, what to make the bed from? The funeral director said how a bed could be made from straw that would be inserted into a long cloth bag and sloped so that the feet would be pointed downward. Then the bed would be made like any other, fitted with a soft white sheet and covered with more fabric and topped off with a pillow.

Inside that old barn Joseph used as his workshop, a thing of beauty was coming together. His wife Helen vigorously shook the tightly compressed sections of the bales to loosen them, releasing more dust and seed into the air. The large cotton bag was filled with straw. All over the community, Prayers for the Dying were said, while preparations for the funeral and meal afterward were made. Michael's choir practiced.

Check-ins with the hospital revealed Michael was losing his battle by the hour; but he was still living. The casket was nearly done, save for the bed. It was time to join everything together. Holding all four corners, the three friends gently lowered the drapes into the newly stained and varnished box. With the rectangular curtain clamped along the top, Joseph securely stapled it in place. Attempts to get a manufactured trim failed, so a finishing touch would have to be found or made for the top of the curtain. A braid developed from gold, cranberry, and brown fabric strips that would hide the staples and be secured with decorative tacks. It was just the perfect touch for the wood grains and warm toned cotton. Everything was in place. One more varnish maybe.

Rita and the children waited and prayed, broken hearted but able to accept God's Will, but never really ready to say goodbye.

"The poor fellow," she would say sadly. Their 2,000-year-old Christian teaching was clear. The mortal body was only the shell that contained the soul, which belonged to God, and it was each one's responsibility to get it back to Him.

Then, the entire project was a thing of beauty and a joy to behold. Joseph would take the beautiful casket to Inverness Funeral Home early the next morning.

Completely finished now, the tired threesome came into the warm family home and put the tea on. Just then, the phone rang; Michael had just passed away. All three just stared at one other, covered in goose bumps. It was Sunday night. It is finished.

The beautiful project was moved to the funeral home early the next morning before Joseph returned to work. Michael's body was laid on the straw bed.

The long wake followed, hundreds and hundreds of people came to honour the man and were in complete awe of his casket. The day of the funeral, Father Duncan watched as Michael's fellow lawyers pranced up the middle aisle, their black gowns billowing behind them, full of air. The bevy of barristers sat together on the left side of the big Catholic Church.

After Mass, Father Duncan started his eulogy with: *"When my mother wanted a lawyer..."* (he panned his finger over the black-robed judges and lawyers in attendance) *"no...she didn't ask for any of you"* he said, *"she wanted Michael!"* A gust of laughter burst out from the sorrowful crowd as he continued *"...and oh no, I was asked to leave!"* More laughter. *"While I drove around, waiting, they were having fresh biscuits and hot tea."*

Welcome laughter continued. *"She loved Michael."* he said, *"Everyone loved Michael."* He spoke of a humble man of great faith, now gone from sight. A lively fiddle tune escorted Michael to the burial ground. But, no grave would hold him; he was already sitting at the Table of the Lord.

The next month, at Easter Mass, the all-female choir was greatly complimented. Just beautiful, they said, but who was the man singing, they asked. They all said he had the voice of an angel.

But, there were no men singing in the choir that day. Except—perhaps one...who stopped by to say, *"I'm still here with you".*

Rest in Peace Michael, who will walk in your footsteps?

The obituary read:

> *Michael Xavier, 51, passed away on Sunday, March 1, 2009, surrounded by his loving family.*

Names have been changed to protect the shy!

GRAMMA MARY CASSIE

A Family Memoir

At the time of this writing, my favourite aunt is 85 and I'm 58. She is widowed and I am divorced. We both enjoy each other's company and have a lot in common, so spending time together suits us just fine. My mother passed away long ago so my aunt's maternal affection is welcome. Her behaviors toward me are akin to mothering; baking, visiting and appreciation of me; her caring and praying for me, and sharing her life's stories. I have always wanted a Gramma and she is the perfect blend of mother and grandmother for me. Colena *never* arrives at my door empty handed: fresh homemade bread or biscuits, lots of homemade soups and her fish cakes are my very favourite!

Her own homemade preserves, cookies, or some other delicious culinary dish is passed to me in clear recycled plastic milk bags. I, in turn, hope I am comparable to a daughter for her, making silly projects and baking Cape Breton oatcakes for her.

I have many other aunts, however I never knew, or know, any of them very well. I care deeply for my Aunt Colena and appreciate all she is and does for me. She has a young spirit about her, is fun and funny. For instance, she suggested it was time to take the 'Burdizzo' (crimper) to a local bishop who was caught in possession of pornographic pictures. The 'Burdizzo', a rough farm instrument that was used

to castrate bulls! I howled in delight and agreed we should find one some-where! 'The crimper' she would say every now and then, shaking her head in disgust! We go many places and do many things that are exciting to us.

For example Sunday Feb 28th, 2010 was the last day of the Olympics in Canada. The U.S. and Canada played each other for the hockey gold medal. Aunt Colena came to my place for the game. As she came in the door, she put her hand in her coat pocket and pulled out her traveling 'flask' and it was then she realized she had forgotten her driver's license. Hugging her tightly I said, *"Great! Eighty-five, no license and open liquor!"*

We pulled two rocking chairs beside the heat of the wood stove and put our feet up. We drank her Baileys Irish Cream on the rocks. She prayed the Rosary in Gaelic and I swore. We were both nervous wrecks, we couldn't even sit down for the last period of overtime. She was **sure** they would lose. I was unable to believe they **could** lose. This was **our** year, **our** Olympics and we had to win; we just **had** to win, especially against our favourite rivals, the United States! Rotating between praying and swearing, we both watched the game on television, hardly breathing.

Then—it happened! Young Nova Scotian player, Sidney Crosby scored the famous golden goal! Canada won the game, we both yelped, jumped around and cried watching Canada receive gold medals. We had quite a time watching the red and white Canadian flag as it was elevated and hearing the words of *Oh Canada*. What a great moment for us. We were so damn proud to be Canadian and so glad to be together for that historic moment!

Colena was one of 6 girls in her family of 17 children; where all the other girls were older except the baby, Annie. So my aunt has lots of memories about her older sisters while they still lived at home and after they got married. She often told me how hard some of her sisters' lives had been. Together we visited two of those sisters in the Inverness Hospital.

Aunt Janet at 91 has neither an ache nor a pain and needs no medication; however, she is totally blind. Unable to live alone now, she currently stays in hospital awaiting a room in the Manor. With too much idle time on her hands sometimes, she gets emotional thinking about her life.

Janet was the third-oldest child and second-oldest daughter. She and Colena both saw their share of diapers and scrubbing before Janet went to live and work at her aunt's place when she was only 15. Janet still resents how much hard work she had to do there. Her paternal aunt, Margaret Isabel (Maggie Belle), kept a boarding house for grade 12 boys going to school at the Mabou convent; the house is still standing on Back Street. Janet worked for this woman for four years, waking up early to make three fires and many breakfasts, before going to school herself; then working after school till midnight. Constantly belittled by the woman, Janet often had to go around the community gathering pieces of wood for firewood for kindling. One time her father and brother came upon her hauling a huge pile of wood back to her aunt. Feeling sorrow for his daughter, Papa returned with a few boxes of split wood for Janet but the bossy aunt refused to use it, saving it instead in the barn. Janet, very strong from the work, was forced to continue working as hard as before. The aunt died with the kindling still stored in the barn!

Even though the aunt ran a boarding house it was Janet who was responsible for meals, cleaning, housework, doing the wash, scrubbing, waxing and polishing floors to all hours. Janet was only allowed to go home for the month of August because the month of July was set aside for totally cleaning the house after all the boys left. Sadly she explained how *"Papa came to take me home on Christmas Eve but the old woman wouldn't let me go home"*.

Janet said her aunt was very bossy and thought of herself as a big shot; that even Janet's father was intimidated and wouldn't disagree with his sister. Janet's mother Mary Cassie believed that her sister-in-law was properly feeding and clothing Janet. Mary Cassie needed her daughter at home with so many other children and probably didn't know how awful life was for her child. But truth be told, Janet toiled and slaved for $2 a month all that time. Janet said that she cried so much when she was at Maggie Belle's that it's any wonder she went blind.

Janet just cannot stop talking about the hard years with her aunt, and the really tough time she had there, not even allowed to walk on the floors she had just polished. The woman got a carpenter and built an apparatus for Janet to hoist herself up through a hole in the ceiling so she would not walk on the freshly polished stairway and floors. She had to open the hatch in the ceiling with her head and crawl up instead of walking on the stairs. Material things were more important than people to that aunt. Janet admits she finally suffered what would be considered a nervous breakdown by the time she left there. She was worked like a slave from the ages of 15 to 19 years. Her breaking point came one day and she simply walked away, in a storm. She walked every step of the way home to Glengarry, refusing to go back.

Janet later married, had a large family and was widowed young. Later in life she lost two sons in the same year. As children, we loved to see Janet come to our house because we were guaranteed some hearty laughs and some of her good homemade cooking! Janet still has great clarity of mind and a pretty feisty spirit. She cannot be fooled on any count, anymore. How sad it makes me to see her cry about her circumstances when she should have been so carefree.

The other sister we visited is Cassie, who also has macular degeneration plus Alzheimer's disease. She cannot see very well and cannot retain my name for more than one whole minute. Yet she has very clear recollections of her childhood in Glengarry and speaks perfect Gaelic. Every time I tell her I am her niece she is shocked and asks who my parents are! Every time I tell her which of her brothers is my father she is shocked again and quickly asks me *"...who did he marry?"* So, I tell her again who my mother is and immediately she sees very clear memories of my mother, Annie Margaret, and praises her ability to work and to cook. Then it starts all over again with the well-rehearsed ritual: *"...and who are you?"* And as we talk, I am well aware they are the prototype of my own aging process.

So we visit. I do what I can to speak loudly, place things in their hands, bring tea and have sincere respect for their histories. This day Cassie talks about how Mama always made mincemeat and fruitcakes at Christmastime how much work they were to make, and how good they were.

Like most of the Scottish families, the large MacDonell/Cameron family was resolutely Roman Catholic. Feast days and fast days were strictly adhered to, not one drop of food or water was to be ingested from midnight the night before in order to receive Communion the following day. Such was the respect they had for the Holy Eucharist. Failure to obey meant Confession was necessary before attending Mass and a severe penance from Father MacPherson or Father MacMaster for breaking the ruling. Colena told me she got up as usual for Mass one time and packed the huge lunch her famished family would eat on the way home, with the horse and sleigh. With no ill intent, the child then innocently drank a mouthful of water. When she realized her crime, she told on herself to her dismayed parents. Too late to go to Confession before Mass, it was not permissible for her to go at all so she went back to bed *"...and was I ever glad"* she said, *"...it was so cold out that day"*. She took the cat and went back upstairs to bed. No Baptized child had any reason not to go to Mass or Communion, especially during the long Easter vigils and *"...many was the time...we all walked, bellies growling, feeling faint and then walked home again"*. Still feeling rebellious, she said it was the only time she ever missed Mass.

After seeing her sisters, Colena always talks about life in Glengarry growing up as a young girl. I decided to record her memories of living in beautiful Glengarry as one of 6 girls and 11 boys where life was no vacation. It was a lifestyle of continuous, never ending labour where the girls helped out, both in the house, barn and fields in every way. No coaxing was necessary for Colena to talk as memories flooded about events and people in her life and childhood. She had particular memories from approximately the mid-'30s, just several years before the Second World War began when she was about age 13 or 14 years old. She talked fondly about her mother ('Mama'), all the babies, food ration coupons, trading flour and making soap. Even with some fun times as an adult member of a big family, she talked not so fondly about the amount of work and how the good old days were just a lot of extremely hard work.

Despite that work, the large family enjoyed winter evenings with *"... Mama and the girls sitting by the stove, knitting. Using the yarn she had spun during the day and the girls making mittens or winding yarn while the boys sat around the table smoking, playing cards and telling stories"*.

Colena rambled on about many topics: like how Gaelic was the primary language spoken; Mama always made soap from ashes; the girls cleaned the sheared wool in the river; the Rosary was said every single evening while Papa said the Litany in English; Mary Cassie and Johnny John had 17 children together and held a huge twenty-fifth wedding anniversary party

in their home; several wakes had taken place there too; 19 babies were born in that house; Colena's brother Donald went overseas; her sister Margie died. Colena had a story to tell and I got out my pencil.

My aunt Colena's father was John Andrew MacDonell[3], son of Margaret 'Peggy' Beaton and John MacDonell[3]. Her was called 'Johnny John The Weaver' or 'Johnny 17'. The MacDonells were styled as 'The Weavers', a label that had come along with the family when they emigrated from Scotland. Colena's mother was Mary Catherine 'Cassie' Cameron. She was the daughter of Mary Campbell and Donald 'Big Dan' Cameron[3], known as 'the Dancer'. Indeed Mary Cassie could 'clip er off', dancing lightly to the sounds of Don Messer's fiddle on the radio. Colena was the eighth child of Papa who was a great farmer, and of Mama who was an exemplary Christian mother. I too, am a MacDonnell Weaver. However, I

[3]A.D MacDonald, *Mabou Pioneers, Volume I, A genealogical tracing of some pioneer families who settled in Mabou and District,* Formac Publishing Company Limited, Halifax, 2014, 880 pages. Chapter XX: The Camerons, pg. 246, Chapter XXIX: MacDonells, South West Mabou, pgs. 614-615, 617-618. Previous editions: 1950, 1952, 1977, 1980, 1998

am particularly interested in my grandmother, and her life in the domestic roles of wife and mother.

Emotionally, my aunt always recalls what a wonderful woman her mother was, and how hard she worked. Tiny, tough and smart, Mary Cassie worked from the moment she awoke, her thick wavy hair wrapped in a little bun. Unpretentious, Colena recalls how  her mother was an energetic and virtuous woman, the epitome of the word Mother. She could make or fix anything, always had a solution for every problem, could spin wool so fine it would fit in the knitting machine, knit, weave, cook, bake, make soap and cheese, and work in the fields if need be. Never one to take a rest, she might kneel for an hour or more slightly leaning on the lounge and pray—if she got a chance. Except for Sundays, at all other times she wore a long white apron that wrapped right around her and tied in the front, cooking while tending to a child or children. It seemed to the child Colena that Mary Cassie was *always* pregnant and indeed she was for 20 years. The oldest child John A. was 19 years old when Baby Annie was born. Babies were born in Mary Cassie's own bed in her bedroom off the kitchen. The local mid-wife, Mrs. Janet Beaton (Alexander the Asylum's mother) usually came to assist. As well, Mary Cassie's sister, Jessie Agnes, served as a midwife in the area for many years and would, if she could, come to her sister's aid in delivery. Indeed, she was no stranger to birthing babies, as she'd delivered 12 of her own. The resulting families have dozens of cousins. Then Doctor Kennedy would be called and he would deliver the babies, if he arrived on time.

"Glengarry has the most beautiful view in the whole world and we didn't even know it" Colena told me, *"...people used to come and Papa would take them up over the hills to see the scenery, taking pictures of the hills and the ocean water from West Mabou, Mabou Harbour and North East Mabou and*

everywhere else". Until she left Cape Breton herself, Colena could never understand their appreciation of the scenery.

I asked about her childhood home and I was very surprised to find the Weaver homestead was so large and spacious. Colena explained: *"...there was a huge main floor, the kitchen was very large with a large porch and pantry, a stairway and then the upstairs: the bedrooms and the loft and then the loom was in the same area where the boys slept. There was a large linen closet upstairs with shelves in it, and a big wide door with wide, wide door frames and hooks to hang up the clothes, especially Sunday clothes. Another open area on the bedroom level (above the kitchen, porch and pantry) was certainly big enough to put several beds in it. It had two big windows and John A. used to put the kerosene lamp on the table there to do his studies. All these areas were finished with plaster, except where the loom was. The house had two brick chimneys, one for the kitchen stove and one for the sitting room where two stoves used the same flue..."* Especially on Sundays, a fire was made in the dining room and always at Christmas. Colena thinks there was a lot of land, many acres, maybe even 300 acres.

"The kitchen was at one end of the house...it was a really large kitchen" she said *"...with a table that would sit 12 people easy with a good size pantry and a good size porch"*. I loved the imagery this description gave me: *"There was always a barrel filled with flour in the pantry with a bread board set on it for kneading the dough. When the bread making was finished, the bread board was turned upside down on the flour barrel to make a table"*. I could see how it could then be used to do other domestic chores like peeling and chopping. And visualize the oven that usually had bread cooking in it and smell the aroma of loaves and loaves of cooling bread. With noticeable regret my aunt grieves at not having some little memento from her first home.

Besides the large kitchen, there was a big living room, sitting room, dining room and bedroom 'down below' on that first floor. Mary Cassie and Johnny John had their bedroom off the kitchen, where the 17 children were conceived.

The house also had *"...four bedrooms upstairs with large walk-in clothes closets in each"*. The oldest of the children slept there in two bedrooms and the girls also shared two bedrooms. One of the girls' bedrooms was called the 'new bedroom' (pronounced 'bedam ooudd' in Gaelic) that could quickly be converted into a spare room for any visitors. Then there was also a large loft that was the size of the kitchen, the porch and the pantry. 'The boys', eight of them at a time, slept there. When one boy left home, another boy gladly took his spot!

"There was a huge unfinished area upstairs where a large bed frame with a clap board base was. The base was covered with a thick supply of straw on it and then the woolen bedclothes went over that. The area easily could have fit four or six beds but there were just layers of straw, no mattresses. Every Christmas the straw was changed in the beds and everyone had a good fresh clean bed for Christmas. Everyone put a long heated stick of wood in their bed in the evening to heat the bed before they got in it". My aunt said she always took the cat (piseag) too!

Among her memories, Aunt Colena can easily recall that every family was allotted coupons or food stamps during the war years. Her family received a larger ration because there were seventeen children. However, the large farming family was living quite self-sufficiently off the land so they didn't need a lot of food stamps for supplies apart from molasses, sugar and tea. One fall, among other vegetables, the family put over one hundred barrels of white and blue potatoes in the cellar. In its day the Weaver farm was an enviable resource.

"Papa always had wheat..." Colena described how he then mowed and helped convert to oatmeal and whole-wheat flour, providing ample food for his large family. Mama always had fresh bread made and huge suppers for her husband and children. As well, people came and traded flour with Mary Cassie.

The odd looking Waterloo stove sat in the kitchen where a large cast iron frying pan, kettle, pot and clothes irons were eternally in use. Thick burlap bags filled with a recent yield of wheat were set behind the stove, stacked about three high to a total of twelve, and continuously rotated so the backs of the bags would dry equal to the front. Colena said they reached nearly to the loft.

Then after a month or so, the bags were taken with the horse, Tilley, on the wood sled to Beaton's Mill in Glenora Falls. There, a local fellow refined it into oatmeal, all-bran and whole-wheat flour. Then more bags of wheat replaced the original batch behind the stove *"...because one round of flour was not going to do for the year"*. Renowned for the constant supply, people often came to Johnny John the Weaver's place with lard cans filled with white flour to trade for whole-wheat flour. The white flour added some moisture and softness to the hard whole-wheat bread and the whole-wheat flour added some fiber and substance to the white bread. The always generous and humble Mary Cassie also gave out their food stamps to anyone who wanted them.

Wheat was referred to as a Gaelic word (cruithneachd) that sounded like 'krunniach.' People came to the beautiful Glengarry for a container full of 'cruithneacdh' and also left with precious coupons, useless to the MacDonell family, therefore making a very good barter for both sides.

Seeing her picture, I realized 'Mama' was only the height of my sister Anita or Aunt Colena, five feet, *"...maybe a little smaller"*, a diminutive woman who was always spinning, cooking, cleaning and having babies. My first cousin Janet MacIsaac remembers her and recalls that, upon seeing our grandmother, she intuitively knew she was a nice person.

She had 17 children in all and it was an older sister Rita who finally protested against the doctor who always left a baby every time he came by! Once, seeing the doctor arrive **again** the innocent girls hid behind the door and in Gaelic Rita wondered aloud why in the Name of God he didn't leave the babies at the neighbour, Donald Ban's place because there were never any babies there! In disbelief, Colena could offer no explanation to her older sister as they both questioned the doctor's motives together. But Doctor Kennedy kept coming by and he kept leaving babies in the bedroom with Mama. Although the girls loved the little babies, there were already several more still in diapers, and there was just too much hand washing for Mama and the girls to keep ahead of. There never was a time in 20 years when there were not cloth diapers and rags to be scrubbed by hand and hung somewhere to dry.

Birth control was prohibited by the Church so the very religious couple would never consider it. Even as teenagers then, young people understood very little about reproduction even unto marriage (one woman was given the advice to *"...make up the grocery list while he's doing what is his right"*). There were no Gaelic words for a person's private parts because anything below the waist was never discussed. The girls had come up with the words 'Joey Brown', and when referring to any personal matters '...down there'. And of course, everyone knew what your 'glingan' meant. These words served as a non-gender specific reference to anything below the waist and was often a private joke between the children, especially the girls.

On the topic of sexual matters, I asked Colena about women's choices. She told me that when she married, she learned that a woman never had a good enough reason to refuse sexual intercourse with her husband. If she did, she was not allowed to go to Communion before she confessed her sinfulness to the priest. I researched the information and found it to be true. The priest could sternly remind a woman of her marital 'bed duties' and of the oath of obedience she promised her husband in the Sacrament of Matrimony. Few women had much sex education, however they promised to always be obedient to it in marriage. Neither sickness nor post partum fatigue was considered a good enough reason to deny the man his right to procreate (or at least to practice). Later in life, the daughters understood why Mama would take the horse and buggy to Port Hood, usually with a child to wait with the horse, while she talked at length with Father Donald. *"Mama often had to go see the priest,"* she said, feeling a renewed respect for her long suffering mother and other women of that era. Some women begged the doctor for 'salt peter' to offset the men's sexual appetite. Today as liberated women, my women friends and I are angered and heartbroken for our female ancestors, as we discuss the few choices they had. The males of the Church had created a very powerful and flawless system for each other that encouraged dominant spousal control.

With the current scandals in the Church, Colena now feels they were all lied to and made to *"...dance around like fools doing all these silly things and the priests themselves were doing worse to little boys"*. Never one to mince words, she was cross and heartbroken to see the changes in the world. Still a regular churchgoer, she has relaxed many of the imposed rules that left her with so much guilt all her life. *"Thank God Mama is not here to see what's happening in the Church and Margie too, they believed so strong. Margie was fasting **all** the time, whether she was pregnant or sick or what."* Colena shakes her head as she hears the news about the Bishop, mocking in her deep low Scottish accent *"...time to get out the Burdizzo"*.

Even in hard circumstances, life had its funny moments, and Colena remembered this one. She certainly laughed heartily as she told me. Johnny John was in need of another large water-tight puncheon barrel, and was able to get one from his new son-in-law, Donald. At home, upon further inspection, Johnny discovered there was a full pail or so of molasses still in it. Not one to be wasteful, he poured it out of the new puncheon and took it in the house for his family. Afraid of the possibility of insects in it, the children were apprehensive about eating it. Always one with a solution, Mary Cassie boiled the molasses, which she then put in a clean container. Before long, the children had covered big thick slices of homemade brown bread with the clean molasses, and everyone had a '...good feed'. However, by nighttime, the delicious boiled molasses had created the same effect as an enema and soon it began to stimulate their bowels. Colena laughed heartily remembering the changing of the guard: *"...one leaving the outhouse in the dark and the other going in, and those who didn't make it at all, and every single one leaving a trail of 'cackkkkkkkkhhh' all the way to the outhouse"*. One boy left the putrid trail of diarrhea from the very top of the stairs to the grass outside. Joey Brown was now spoken of in a more serious tone as everyone had a very sore bum from the 'bunnyoch'.

She said every single piece of underwear had brown streaks and there had to be a big wash the day after eating the boiled molasses. Sometimes being frugal had its snags.

Janet met her husband-to-be at a dance at the Port Hood hall. Margie soon invited Janet and Donald MacMillan home for a nice dinner. When she realized there was no dessert, she quickly made a raisin pie. She set it on the window sill to cool while they ate, and got to know Donald. But the family dog saw it there too, and pulled it right off the sill. By the time Margie was ready to serve dessert to her sister and her new boyfriend, the dog had eaten the pie and the hens were pecking at the last of the crumbs. She was very, very, embarrassed.

Margie was the first of the girls to have a child. She went to the hospital in Inverness and her firstborn son was born in December, when there *"...was a terrible big storm"*. Colena was not sure how Margie got to the hospital, but recalled she got there just in time to deliver, and *"...had the 'purtiest' little baby you ever seen..."*. Alex Roderick was born that cold December day, and once released from the hospital Margie went home to Glengarry in January, with her newborn son. She treasured being there with her Mama and sister so much, she didn't even want to go home. Margie had made a make-shift bedroom for herself in the living room, where the wood stove kept her and the baby warm. Margie *"...simply loved her baby Alex Roderick, she simply adored him, holding and kissing him, smiling she would tell him '...you are **my** baby' and was '...kissing and kissing and kissing his little face' she repeatedly told him: '...I love you, love you, **love** you!'"* Aunt Colena said to me *"...Margie was so happy, she was clear in love with that baby, you'd think she never saw a baby before!"*

So Margie came home to Glengarry with her newborn to be helped out and trained by her experienced mother. Colena remembers that during that time, the new mother invited her husband and her sister-in-law, Flora Mae MacDonald, to a huge meal on a Sunday afternoon intending to go home with them after dinner was over. She had made it all herself and it was wonderful, with all the trimmings. But the family 'ceilidh' was cut short because there was a wild winter snow storm brewing and Donald was not accustomed to going through the fields alone. He left quickly on horse and sleigh but Margie wouldn't go out with a new baby plus she wanted to stay home longer.

She stayed so long, her husband Donald finally came by to take his wife and baby home after a month. *"He had a talk with her in the living room"*. *"So Margie left with him that day."* My aunt told me she was sorry to see her sister go home. They were all having such fun with the new baby and the happy Mommy.

Donald was a kind man, a good singer, and people liked his company. Not one to waste money on extravagant things, neighbors offered drinks to get him singing which he would never refuse and soon the singing and card playing would begin. Colena liked Donald because he was a gentle man, and he was nice to her sister Margie. He was not brought up on a farm, and so it was Margie who knew what to do with animals and gardens. He had an education, but there were no jobs anywhere at that time. Papa had given them a cow that was with calf. This was the sort of dowry the father of a bride often gave in those days if he could. When the calf was born, the quick-witted Margie took it indoors from the cold barn. She kept it alive by warming it by the heat on the open oven door.

Margie was soon pregnant again in 1947 with her second child. In July of that year *"...and seven months in a family way"* Margie came home to Glengarry one day to help Mama with house cleaning chores. Colena had been there alone with her mother that day, so together she and Margie began the day's chores. They threw all the wash (including urine stained quilts and *"...the boy's stinky long underwear that had been worn all winter long"*) out the upstairs loft windows. They began soaking them in big galvanized tubs of hot water which they had heated on a fire outside. Then they began the long demanding job of scrubbing by hand on washboards with Mama's homemade lye soap. The soapy water then had to be replaced by clean rinse water, and wringing the soap out of the heavy blankets. Carrying water, scrubbing clothes and *"...hanging all that up on fences, clothes lines and spreading them out on the grass all day"* was very heavy work. Margie went into labour that evening probably due to the strenuousness of it all. *"She 'kept it to herself'"* Colena said about her sister *"who 'stayed quiet' that evening"*. During the night Margie called out to her mother, when it was obvious she was in labour. By then she was nearly ready to deliver.

Even though labour and child birth were common occurrences in Mary Cassie's life, she did **not** make a good midwife. All too familiar with the painful twinges of childbirth, *"...poor Mama got scared and just couldn't stay* *inside the house"*. She ran outside that beautiful summer morning, clasping her hands over her breaking heart. There, distraught and crying, she knelt on the ground and called on all the Saints and Angels in Heaven to help her daughter Margie, especially imploring the aid of the Blessed Mother. Frightened, young Colena went outside to seek help and to soothe her mother, pleading in Gaelic: *"Mama, after all the babies you had, you must know what to do!"* But Mama continued to cry, holler and pray, experiencing so much sympathy for her daughter she became weak from the strain. *"It was just awful, I didn't know what to do"* my aunt recalled.

On horseback, Colena's younger brother Alexander rushed to fetch Dr. MacNeil in Mabou, but Marie Bernice MacDonald was born without him, two months early in the midst of the demanding housecleaning chores. *"Margie came up home to help Mama and left with a baby"* Colena said while still vividly recalling how stressed her mother had become from seeing her daughter in labour. Blaming the heavy work for the early delivery, Colena said there had been no stopping Margie from doing the chores that day. *"She was going to do it anyway..."* Colena said Margie also adored this tiny baby girl as she did her first born.

Therefore it was that very hot summer day when the Choirs in Heaven obeyed Mary Cassie and ushered a beautiful little girl into the world. A space of a few years had passed since the birth of the last child in that house and the novelty of a new baby was, by contrast to Mama's reaction, a very joyful experience. Both Margie and Colena were elated with the birth of a little girl. Colena said, *"...it was an awful thing to go through but I **loved** that little girl".*

Having missed out on all the excitement of the birth, their youngest brother, Lawrence, realized the bottom drawer was missing from a bureau that day. Coming into the kitchen he was surprised to find it on the kitchen table with a tiny baby in it. *"In the name of God, where did that baby come from?"* he exclaimed. Surely the doctor wasn't going to start leaving babies there again!

Home births were not uncommon in those days, however obstetrics were still quite primitive. Margie always told her sister how she *"...never felt good a single day..."* after that birthing. Without question, gynecology and obstetrics being advanced as they are today, we can safely believe that Margie retained some degree of infection that lay undetected but active for many years. Further pregnancies failed to flush it out and eventually it caused her death. The very name of their sister Margie evokes hurt and sadness from the many siblings who loved this creative and incredibly smart hard-working woman. Colena told me many times: *"Margie could do anything, make anything out of nothing, wasted nothing, birthed calves, had a beautiful garden, did carpentry, cooked meals, loved to sing, tell stories and loved to have people in and...well...she was really something else".* I take great pride when Colena compares both Mary Janet and myself to her sister Margie. Colena still regrets her early passing saying it was such a shame, believing Margie to be a saint in Heaven. Indeed we all feel gypped we did not know her.

When Janet (Colena's sister) went into labour with Gerard there was a raging snowstorm and she could only make it as far as Glengarry. She delivered Gerard there upstairs and said all Mama could do was get on her knees and pray and cry! Janet said that after having seventeen children of her own Mama wasn't much good to her!

Changing topics to something more pleasant, I asked my aunt where her mother got the soap for doing the wash. She said, *"...Mama always made the soap",* and I pressed her for memories of that process.

"Well", she said, as the images became clearer in her mind, *"we had to save the ashes from the wood stove all winter in a pile outside, and we had to save the 'drippings' of any meat or use tallow from butchering".* *"That's what we used to make soap, every year, in the spring"* she said, *"Mama always made the soap, and when I helped her, I ran around and got things for her. The other girls might have different memories of helping her. But I remember she always made it outside in the spring, in a big pot over a **good** fire".* *"Rainwater was gathered in a puncheon by leaning a stick or branch from the roof and it guided the water into the puncheon. As compared to the pump water, we called it 'soft water' so Mama used soft puncheon water to make the soap".*

The soap making procedure was two-fold and usually took two days. Fat and lye were needed but they had to be made. First the tallow and/or fat drippings were boiled in rain water in a big pot the day before the actual soap was made. This part could be done inside the house. A huge pot was filled with water and the fat and drippings were dumped in it and boiled. I researched tallow boiling where the rind of the meats and particles of food separated from the drippings during the boiling process. Then these dregs and scum were usually given to the hens because everything was used and nothing was wasted. Women had to be thinking carefully to work the season's bounties, cautiously planning in order to have the necessary elements when the time was right. Tallow was gathered in the fall butchering, and ashes followed winter's heating to be ready for spring which was soap making time.

Colena recalls bringing the necessary water to her mother. It had been saved in the large tubs they called 'puncheons'. Then the hot boiled grease was collected from the pot in the kitchen. Mary Cassie probably poured the water through a sieve or cloth, because as Colena said, *"...we had very good clean soap."*

Lye had to be coaxed out of the hardwood ashes *"...the ashes from the wood stove always had to be saved in a pile outside...like you see gravel piled in a heap"*. In the spring, some ashes would be sifted to remove any chunks of unburnt pieces of wood, nails, wires or any rubbish. Then really hot water was poured through the sifted ashes. Colena does not remember what container the ashes would be put in for this process, however most pioneer homes had a homemade wooden apparatus called a 'hopper' which held the ashes while the water was poured over it and leaked out through a hole or spigot in the bottom. The hot water soaked the ashes and the resulting liquid came out as lye. This lye, necessary for soap making, was sometimes just skimmed off somehow and set aside in a pail or iron container. Lye was dangerous to the touch.

While some of my aunt's memories were limited when it came to exactly how soap was made it makes sense that fat and lye were cooked together to make soap. She knew running hot water through wood ashes created soda or alkaline called lye. I wondered if my Gramma Mary Cassie knew the physics of that process or was she simply doing what someone else had shown her to do? Another thing I wondered about my grandmother Mary Cassie: did she make the soap alone (except for a little runner girl) to protect her children, because she knew lye would burn if it touched the skin and damage the lungs if inhaled? Making it outside prevented her children from touching or inhaling any of it. My heart pounds proudly and my nose starts to tingle as I learn about this wonderful woman but I ache with sadness as I wish I had known her.

Colena could not recall what else her Mama had sent her running for every time but it may also have been salt as some homemade soap had salt added. My research told me that towards the end of the boiling time, salt was added by the handful to bind the ingredients into a solid mass. But she was still a child then and cannot recall that point today. All she understood was that her Mama knew what she was doing and she obediently obeyed her orders. At another time, another sibling probably helped make soap, and their recollections are probably much the same but with some new information.

The caustic lye from the ashes and the greasy water from the tallow now had to be added together and boiled in a huge cast iron pot, where the two ingredients would create soap. Outside, Colena's mother set the pot into a hot, hot fire, using soft water again from the puncheon. Liquid lye was added, followed by the fat, and then the salt. The mixture boiled while being stirred continuously to avoid over-boiling. It was necessary to watch the boiling ingredients with great care for signs of thickening. If it got too thick the soap was ruined. Colena envisioned her mother holding the big long-handled spoon high up in the air, and the liquid soap threading to a thin string to the pot. As soon as it began to thicken ('chew'), Mary Cassie removed the heavy pot from the fire and allowed the contents to cool for a time. She must have been a powerfully strong woman. When the soap was cool, it was poured into big black pans, probably used to cook rolls and roasts at another time. They had to be very clean Colena told me. Then, all that remained to be done was to cut the clear yellow cakes into long rectangular blocks and put them in pails or tin cans somewhere where rodents would not eat them. These all-purpose bars were used for scrubbing wooden floors, doing laundry, washing hair and taking baths. *"Mama made very good soap".*

Again, with sadness and pride, Aunt Colena remembered the long days of endless work when her mother sacrificed every day for her family. My Gramma, Mary Cassie Cameron/MacDonell. I am so proud to say I am Mary Cassie's granddaughter.

During shearing time the MacDonell girls took all the sheep, 30 or so, to the brook and let them wade in the water where they washed them with the lye soap. Upon returning home, the sheep were then sheared, and Maggie Anne (Mary Cassie's sister) was the one for that job as *"...she was as strong as any man...she would grab the sheep right by the back, flip it over and in no time, it was bare-naked".* The shorn wool was taken to the brook and washed again, only not on the sheep anymore. The girls took the heavy bags of wool, a huge pot, a lunch, and made a fire. They picked it clean of twigs and leaves, then washed the heaps of greasy wool again in the hot water and soap. They laid it all out to dry on the bank beside the river. The next day, the girls would go back to the riverside and turn the wool over, to dry on the other side. Some they would take home. From there, the bundles of wool were sent away to PEI, where it would be cleaned and blown into bundles of what looked like furry batting. When it returned on the train, Mary Cassie and other women gathered together for a carding bee. They then spun their share into yarn. The girls remember (as I do myself) holding my hands straight out so the mother could wrap the skeins into balls of yarn.

Whenever Mary Cassie got a chance she sat at the loom and wove. I have a fascination with looms and shuttles and once took several courses on weaving. So I know that loading the loom is a long tedious process. For my grandmother, it could only be done during the day when the sunlight came into the loft. Mary Cassie, gentle soul that she was, showed her daughter Colena how to push the shuttle back and forth to create a blanket. Colena never knew if she did it correctly because her mother never scolded her.

Always proclaiming her mother to be a saintly person, Colena cannot recall her Mama to ever have been unkind.

Mary Cassie wove many blankets for her children. Colena said she would be so excited when it was time to take the finished product off the loom, and take it to the kitchen to do the final finishing touches. A creative person myself, I admit to knowing that feeling very well. I only wish I had a piece of her weaving to touch, hold close to my heart and catch her spirit. Regrettably only one blanket that we know of is still in existence and is safely in the possession of her granddaughter Carrie Beaton. I can easily envision Mary Cassie weaving at her loom in the loft, silently praying, and offering any troubles up to God.

I am very fond of my first cousin Mary Janet MacDonald. We were born the same day of the same year and have remained close friends all our lives. Colena tells me that Mary Janet looks very much like her father's mother Jessie Belle Beaton. She also says we are both very much like her own mother and her sister Margie: creative, multi-tasking, resourceful, hard-working gals who deal with any issue head on and successfully. I have many other female cousins who fit the same description. True or not, I take it as an enormous compliment to be spoken of in the same vein as all these women.

Colena was very close with Mary Janet's mother Margie. I knew some of the events of Margie's life and death and wanted to hear more details from her. It was very hard for her to speak of her sister so I put my pencil away to honour her feelings. Listening to and seeing her great love I feel I've gotten a true depiction of my other aunt, Margie MacDonald.

Margie was the second child of the seventeen and much like her mother. The older girls had had their fair share of washing diapers and changing babies before they ever had their own. A dark haired and beautiful lass, Margie learned early all the skills necessary for family life, making her very resourceful and smart. She was going to need all the expertise she could get, as life was not to be without its troubles for her.

When Donald MacDonald proposed to her, his father had a success-ful business as a store owner in Mabou where he sold essentials such as molasses, tea, and kerosene. It appeared to Mary Cassie that Margie would have enough comforts of home and the essentials of life to not have to work as hard as she did.

Prior to the marriage taking place Donald's father died, leaving Donald as the proprietor of the store. However, times were hard for everyone then. The store closed but Donald and Margie got married as planned, and faced their future, be what it may. They had to move in with Donald's mother, and his sister Flora Mae, at Alex Donald Cross' house in Mabou. As babies came along, the capable and resourceful Margie, who had grown up spinning, knitting and cooking while caring for endless babies sometimes filled the role as mother and provider. She planted a garden right outside the back door, where she could tend to it, and pluck from it while making sure her children were safe.

First born to Margie and Donald was Alex Roderick, the baby Margie adored and kissed so much, then Bernice arrived on wash day in summer. Margie loved each one like the first, kissing, hugging and holding them near her whenever she could. John Donald and Francis Lawrence were born in that order. From the very start, little Francis seemed to have trouble swallowing and eating and he cried a lot. Colena said the milk just dribbled from his mouth onto his chin. As days went on it seemed as though the poor baby would starve to death if he didn't eat soon. Overcome, Margie took the hungry child and the other children 'up home' to get her family to help rock him. Weeks passed; the tiny newborn got thinner and weaker by the day. One month old, infant Francis Lawrence died from starvation. It was a blockage in his esophagus, which didn't allow the milk to pass through. Today it is a simple operation, but not then. He is buried on the graves of his grandparents.

Today, a doctor's examination/diagnose would have been followed shortly by inserting a feeding tube in his stomach, and the problem would soon be repaired in a minor procedure. But then, Margie painfully witnessed the life slowly fade from her baby as she watched helplessly. While Francis Lawrence was on this earth, he was taken perfect care of while Margie and Donald loved him to death.

Colena described the christening gown the tiny infant was waked and buried in. It was the same one she and her siblings had been baptized in. Mary Cassie had taken very good care of it, cleaning it when necessary and replacing it in the same box after each use, so it was still in good condition, even after seventeen Baptisms. It was a very long, beautiful white dress, which also had a long slip, lengthy coat and bonnet. It had scalloped, embroidered edges on what looked like a quilted coat. Colena thought it had come from Boston and hasn't seen anything quite like it since then. By stark contrast, the beloved little baby in the casket was unusually brown, and startlingly undernourished, as he was waked in the lovely little outfit. The parents were devastated and *"...it sure was a hard, hard time for Margie"*. After 17 joyful trips to the local church for Baptisms, the gown is now buried in Mabou, with a little saint in it. The child was buried on top of his own grandfather's grave instead of being set aside alone.

Soon Margie was expecting Mary Janet. This child too came into the world in a severe snowstorm. Margie and Donald were taken to the hospital in a storm by taxi driver and fiddler Donald Angus Beaton. Margie arrived at the hospital just in time to deliver. Her sister-in-law, Annie Margaret, (my mother) also made the hurried trip to the hospital that night too, quickly delivering a girl who would be named Donelda. Fifty-eight years later, I am that same individual who is writing my aunt's recollections.

Whenever she got a ride, Margie travelled to Glengarry or would go by horse and sleigh taking her children: Alex Roderick, as she always called him, Bernice, John Donald and baby Mary Janet with her. She would come, like she did the day Bernice was born, to help her mother in any way she could be of assistance because it was obvious Mama was now very sick.

Mary Cassie finally succumbed to her pain and fell down in her own kitchen. She knew she was dying with cancer. In 1952 every one of Mary Cassie's children had come home for Christmas, knowing their mother would not live to see another one. After Christmas all went back to where they had come from, except Colena. Mary Cassie asked her daughter to stay with her because she needed her help, knowing she was dying, and realizing *"Papa could do nothing"*. So Colena had written her husband,

Bernie MacMillan in Windsor, Ontario, to say she was going to stay home with Mama 'till she would pass away. Johnny John was very sad for his wife's suffering.

The daughters in the family helped care for their mother during the last months of her life. Two sisters were pregnant and they still came every other day. Janet was expecting Greg and Margie was expecting Bernie G. Their Mama lay dying in her bed day after day, and though she never complained, they all knew she was in a lot of pain. She had cancer in her womb and Colena had little experience in helping her. Alone with her, she devised a make-shift means of turning her mother on a bed sheet. *"Poor Mama suffered so much and I didn't know what to do, I gave her milk by the spoonful. Maybe it was the wrong thing to do, I don't know"*. Trying to relieve my aunt's regret about her inability to help, I offered my opinion that it was too late then for a cure at that point and Mary Cassie was no doubt fasting to further purge her soul from sin. Catholics often are known for accepting their pain while offering it up to God to defer their sinfulness to avoid prolonged suffering in Purgatory. The priest would come every once in awhile and anoint Mary Cassie with what's known as the Sacrament of Extreme Unction. She would stare fixated at pictures of the Blessed Mother and Sacred Heart of Jesus, pleading with God to forgive her for all her sins, spreading her hands open wide to measure the amount *"...Iosa, Madie (Jesus and Mary), think of the one with **no** sins asking for forgiveness!"* Colena would say to me. I was growing more and more aware of the great saint my grandmother is.

"Mama only asked for water, she ate nothing and was in terrible pain for months". She asked Colena to stay *"...till this is over"* and said, *"...I know what this is. I know I'm not going to get better and I'd like for you to stay with me 'till this is over"* advising her about the dress she would wear in her casket and revealing her wishes for the family to pray. Every night whoever was around prayed the Rosary by her bedside. Because the older girls Cassie and Rita were living away, Colena and Margie were there a lot together.

One day in January, Margie took Colena behind a door so they could talk privately. Margie whispered the word 'buddalin' and indeed Colena knew what she meant because the care of her mother involved putting oil on her mother's private parts. Mary Cassie's womb was actually growing outside of her body, and Colena told her sister that. Then Margie showed her sister a pair of her own underwear and there was a strange liquid mark on it. Margie wanted to know if it was similar to her mother but Colena didn't know, both mother and daughter being too shy to look. Trembling, Margie revealed to her sister that she too had been told she had the dreaded cancer. Colena said they were both very upset *"...but I didn't want her to see me crying...and I thought of the dear little kids Margie loved so much and the husband who needed her and how she would suffer like Mama"*. The girls and their Mama were so shy about such personal matters; they didn't know what to say to each other.

Margie explained how she had gone to see Dr. Guzidol, in West Bay Road by taxi driven by (Long) Duncan Rankin. Sharing the fare, five women had gone that day because all five were expecting. Upon examination, the doctor immediately told Margie *"...right there that day she had cancer"* because he knew what the discharge meant. I try to put myself in her place and panic takes over and tears come to my eyes. What a horrible thing for her to experience. I envision the young beautiful women Margie and Colena, two young un-informed sisters looking at each other behind their mother's bedroom door as she lay dying in the bedroom. The awful news settled into their minds and hearts. Margie did not want her Mama to know she was sick but Colena thinks Mama instinctively knew something was wrong. She kept saying, *"...I hope Margie gets along alright"*. Margie ought to have gone to Glace Bay right then to get treatments but opted instead to stay behind and help her mother.

Colena slept in the bed with her mother, who ate nearly nothing because she could not swallow without choking. Her eldest son, John A. came by every single evening. There were no telephones but he sent telegram messages to family across Canada from the Mabou Railway Station.

In February 1953, little Mary Janet celebrated her first birthday in Glengarry with her mother and grandmother who were both ill. Margie would come up home and bring her youngest baby, Mary Janet, with her. *"Margie made a nice birthday cake so quickly, I didn't even see her put it together."* Colena told me. *"Then she put a little match, or something, in it for a candle"* for the beautiful little child turning one year old. Margie had been feeding the little one baby food that came in small tin cans. Colena asked her if she could have an empty can for cutting out biscuits. Margie willingly agreed and opened the other end of it for her. Fifty-eight years later, Colena still has the same little can even though it has travelled to Windsor and back again. She makes biscuits every other day and has for many years, and every single time, *"I think of Margie and Mary Janet"* her sister and the little girl who turned one the day it was opened. *"I even used it today"* she told me and I knew she had, because she passed me fresh whole-wheat biscuits in clear recycled plastic bags when she came in my door. She plans to give it to Mary Janet someday.

Life went on as usual; children were tended to, Mama was cared for, meals were made, and prayers were said. Continuously asking in prayer for forgiveness for her sins, Mama lingered silently in pain. Bed bound and uncomfortable, she asked to have her hair cut for the first time in her life. Colena cut her hair and still regrets not saving it as a keepsake. Margie and Donald had to make a decision about who would take care of the baby while Margie would go for cancer treatments. They chose Margaret Anne Beaton, one of Mary Cassie's sisters. So one day, Colena dressed and held the heavily wrapped child, as Margie drove the horse and sleigh to Maggie Anne's house across the frozen ice. Mary Janet would be brought up there.

Once there and very upset, the adults had the important conversation in the Beaton kitchen. Her aunt Maggie Anne agreed to raise the child with her own children. Even though the conversation was in both English and Gaelic, and even though she could not speak, the beautiful child understood she was going to be staying there with Maggie Anne. Stopping her play on the kitchen floor, Mary Janet carefully approached her mother, and crawled into her lap. Staring at the people present, she seemed to be saying, *"I want to stay with Mommy"*. Still sadly recalling the day, Colena wipes fresh tears away as she says to me, *"...Margie cried and cried and cried, all the way there and back...I thought she'd get a cold and be sick, tears freezing on her face."* she said. *"Leaving there that day was a really, really hard thing to do".*

Maggie Anne would be known as 'Mama' to Mary Janet, with whom she would live until her marriage to Cecil MacDonald, from Port Hood. It was one of Maggie Anne's daughters, Minnie, who taught Mary Janet to step dance. Minnie also happens to be Natalie MacMaster's mother.

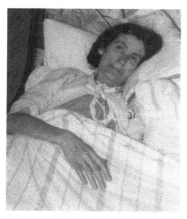

With Mary Janet settled, Margie should have gone to Glace Bay then, but she opted instead to stay with her mother, and help Colena to care for her in her dying days. Meanwhile *"...Mama just got smaller and smaller in the bed".*

During the evening of March 17th, 1953, siblings Lawrence, Little Annie, and Colena were all together, praying in their mother's room with their father, and Catherine Anne Gillis. The aroma of lit candles filled the room. It was Little Annie's seventeenth birthday, the seventeenth child, and it was March 17. Johnny John swept a Blessed candle over and around his wife, over and around again, repeating the Prayers of the Dying, while Colena sprinkled Holy Water on her and everyone prayed together. These were important practices of the Catholic Church, done in earnest to keep the devil from snatching a soul as it passed. Those present knew Mary Cassie was in the final moments of her life, so they prayed continuously, as they cried for losing her. Into the morning hours, Mary Cassie continued to fade away from this world. After some time, *"Mama just lifted her head a little bit off the pillow, and a little drool came from her mouth. She put her head back down again and died. March 18th, 1953 'straight into Heaven'"* Colena said, *"Mama was a saint while she lived and she is a saint now. She had a very peaceful death".* As far as Colena can remember, it was Little Annie and Catherine Anne Gillis who washed Mary Cassie's body, dressed her in the chosen dress, and put her in the casket that John A. had gotten at Fred Hunt's Store, in Mabou. Soon my Gramma was being waked in another room, the family keeping all night vigil, praying as long as her spirit would linger, usually considered to be three days. *"Mama looked so beautiful, just so peaceful. She had such a beautiful death".* So many years later, Colena still mourns her wonderful mother.

Only then did Margie go to Glace Bay for radiation therapy. The doctor administering the treatment had to reach inside and turn the baby's body so that his face would be away from the radiation, but as soon as he would turn it, the baby would flip back, making it necessary for the procedure to be done again. Once Margie reached the seventh month, it was decided to do a Caesarian section, so chemotherapy treatment could begin. Thus, Bernie Gerard (Bernie G.) was delivered prematurely by C-section.

Margie's sister Cassie took care of the newborn for a few months, then her aunt, Sarah Anne (Mary Cassie's sister) took him for good. Colena said Donald MacDonald wanted the baby boy to be brought up at home in Mabou, so he'd be closer to him and the rest of the children. Alex Roddie, Bernice, and John Donald were already in school and were able to remain at home with their father and his sister, Flora Mae.

So, regrettably, Colena could not take the infant, even though she wanted to. Despite all the recent grief in her life, Colena made her life in Windsor. Years later, Colena's husband Bernie got a job at the mill in Port Hawkesbury, and they moved back home anyway. Colena recalls that Margie died on September 4th of 1955, living over three years after Bernie G's birth. She suffered with cancer when she came home, with pain so severe she could be heard from Mabou in her agony. Margie is buried in the Mabou cemetery.

My aunt Colena is now in her mid-90s and living in a rest home in Antigonish because she can no longer live alone. I'm so glad she poured out her memories to me so long ago and that I took the time to listen. How many times have you heard people state, *"I wish I had taken the time to listen to what Mama had to say."* Please, take the time.

Donelda MacDonnell

AFTERWORD

heroes and heroines come in many forms for many various accomplishments: Sports players achieve greatness amid the financial ability to do so; movie stars donate millions when it doesn't spoil their lifestyle one bit; politicians reward themselves for less than admirable work. We need some new heroes. We need some saints around us. I feel I have known a few, whose footsteps I couldn't even step into. These people have threaded my tartan heart and I hold them dear. Their lives and sacrifices, their love of faith and music have made me who I am and I love them for that. Surround yourself with people who impress and inspire you.

CAPE BRETON OATCAKES

Photo: Celine Papillon

MIX	1 lb. (2 cups) butter
	1 lb. (2 cups) Golden Crisco vegetable shortening
	2 cups granulated sugar

ADD	1 tsp. baking soda dissolved in a few tablespoons (about 4–5) of boiling hot water
	Swish around in a cup and add to the butter batter
	Mix well

ADD	4 cups rolled oats: Quaker Minute Oats or Quaker Quick Oats
	4 cups all purpose flour
	Mix well

Divide the dough in half and work with one-half at a time. Sprinkle some rolled oats on your counter and roll the dough out flat (to about 1/8" thickness). Sprinkle some rolled oats over the top as well. Cut into squares. For best results, use a metal egg flipper that is really sharp. Not a thick plastic one. Place on an ungreased cookie sheet or a cookie sheet lined with parchment paper. Bake at 325°F for about 12–15 minutes. Repeat with second half of dough. Delicious with a swipe of butter on top when cooled, along with a hot cup of good Cape Breton tea!

PRAYER TO ST. MICHAEL

St. Michael the Archangel, defend us in this day of battle, be our safe-guard against the wickedness and snares of the devil. May God rebuke him, we humbly pray, and do thou, Oh Prince of the Heavenly Hosts, by the power of God, cast down into hell—Satan and all the evil spirits who wander around the world, seeking the ruin of souls. Amen.

ΛBOUT THE ΛUTHOR

Author photo: Steve Rankin Photography

Donelda MacDonnell is an as-yet undiscovered author who graduated from both St. Francis Xavier and Dalhousie universities. She is retired in Port Hood, Cape Breton Island, Nova Scotia. Her artistic side is evidenced by hand-drawn images and quilted pictures, stitched together in harmony with her writing.

Donelda is a well-respected person and seamstress, quick witted and generous to a fault. She is special to her many friends, all of whom can boast of beautiful hand-made items gifted to them. This is her first book of short stories, but probably not her last.

Manuscript coordination: Mary Janet MacDonald

Typesetting, design coordination: M. MacDonnelle, 2M Media

Editing: Duncan MacDonnell, 2M Media

Photography, scanning: Steve Rankin Photography

Cover design: Colin MacDougall, JoePop Images

Weaving tartan heart icon: Colin MacDougall, JoePop Images

CPSIA information can be obtained
at www.ICGtesting.com
Printed in the USA
LVHW070938110921
697464LV00016B/54